Artists in Residence

By Dana Micucci
Photographs by Marina Faust

The Little Bookroom
New York

Text © 2001 by Dana Micucci
Photographs © 2001 by Marina Faust (except where noted)
Design by Katy Homans and Christine N. Moog
Slipcover design by Angela Hederman
Front cover photograph: Studio of Eugène Delacroix, Paris
Back cover photograph: Delacroix's palette
Printed in Hong Kong

ISBN 1-892145-00-6
First Printing April, 2001
Published by The Little Bookroom
5 St. Luke's Place
New York NY 10014
(212) 691-3321
(212) 691-2011 fax
book-room@rcn.com

Library of Congress Cataloging-in-Publication Data
Micucci, Dana, 1961-
    Artists in residence : a guide to the homes and studios of eight
19th-century artists in and around Paris / by Dana Micucci ; photographs
by Marina Faust.
        p. cm.
    "Claude Monet, Charles-François Daubigny, Vincent van Gogh,
Jean-François Millet, Rosa Bonheur, Gustave Courbet, Eugène Delacroix,
Gustave Moreau"--CIP galley t.p.
        Includes biographical references.
        ISBN 1-892145-00-6 (pbk.)
        1. Artists' studios--France--Paris Region--Guidebooks. 2.
Painters--France--Paris Region--Homes and haunts--Guidebooks. 3.
Painting, Modern--19th century--France--Guidebooks. 4. Paris Region
(France) --Guidebooks. I. Title.
    N8520 .M55 2001
    759' .436--dc21
                                                    00-059820
Portions of the chapter on van Gogh were excerpted from the author's
article "Van Gogh at Home in Auvers" in *Art & Antiques*, December, 1993.
Portions of the chapter on Millet were excerpted from the author's article
"Barbizon Revisited" in *Art & Antiques*, September, 1995.
Portions of the chapter on Moreau were excerpted from the author's article
"Moreau's Mystic Genius" in *Art & Antiques*, April, 1994.

Table of Contents

Introduction

Among Vincent van Gogh's own favorite works was the one entitled *Daubigny's Garden*, one of several paintings and sketches he made there. Van Gogh returned again and again, we conjecture, not only because of the garden's physical beauty, but because of its emotional resonance. A setting so infused with the spirit of his esteemed and beloved predecessor must have been deeply significant for the younger artist.

This same impulse draws us to artists' homes and studios. Carefully preserved for more than a century and open to the public, the sites described in these pages offer an intimate glimpse into the private worlds of Claude Monet, Charles-François Daubigny, Vincent van Gogh, Jean-François Millet, Rosa Bonheur, Gustave Courbet, Eugène Delacroix, and Gustave Moreau. Fortunately, most of these residences are only a convenient day trip from Paris (and the homes and studios of Delacroix and Moreau are actually in the city). The scenic villages of Barbizon, Auvers-sur-Oise, Giverny, and Ornans have remained relatively unchanged over the years, enchanting today's traveler with the same natural beauty that so inspired the artists who settled here.

To tread the narrow streets of Auvers-sur-Oise and Giverny, to ramble through the majestic Fontainebleau forest near Barbizon, to wander through the lush hills and valleys of Ornans, and to explore the artists' homes and studios at their center is to feel magically part of their history. Products of the same time and place, the artists in this volume lived lives that crossed paths and intertwined. By visiting their homes, it is our privilege to meet them on terrain that nourishes a personal connection far beyond that afforded by an art museum.

Dana Micucci
July, 2000
New York City

Claude Monet: *Nymphéas:*
Effect du Soir (1897–98),
Musée Marmottan-Claude Monet,
Paris.

Claude Monet

Although he was born in Paris in 1840, Oscar-Claude Monet would be most strongly identified throughout his long life with Normandy, where he moved as a small boy. It was there, in Le Havre, that he attracted the attention of Eugène Boudin, who introduced him to open-air painting. "If I have indeed become a painter, I owe it to Eugène Boudin," Monet acknowledged. "With infinite kindness, he set about my education. Gradually my eyes were opened, and I understood nature; at the same time I learned to love her." In 1859, Monet returned to Paris to study art, enduring the first of many years of financial hardship. After marrying his mistress, Camille Doncieux, he lived in Argenteuil, where he became an influential member of a group that included Renoir, Pissarro, Sisley, Caillebotte, and Manet. In 1874, rebuked by the Salon, Monet helped organize the first independent exhibition of the group. The show ignited a storm of protest from the public and art establishment alike, who denounced the paintings as no more than unfinished sketches. It was Monet's *Impression, Sunrise*, a view of Le Havre harbor with morning fog, that prompted a critic to mockingly dub the rebel group the Impressionists. By 1878, the impoverished artist had returned to Paris, and, in an ongoing effort to reduce expenses, set up house in Vétheuil with his wealthy friends, Alice and Ernest Hoschedé, and their six children. After the bankrupt Ernest abandoned his family, Monet, now a widower, began a relationship with Alice, whom he would later marry. In 1883, the painter discovered the picturesque village of Giverny, where he spent the last half of his life. Here he created some of his most innovative works, many of them inspired by his legendary gardens and water lily pond. By the time of his death, in 1926, he had solidified his reputation as France's greatest landscape painter and, moving beyond Impressionism, established himself as a pioneer of modern art.

Theodore Robinson: *Claude Monet in his garden, cane in hand* (c. 1887), Musée Marmottan-Claude Monet, Paris; Giraudon/Art Resource, New York.

Monet in Giverny
1883–1926
The Color of Light

"If I were settled somewhere permanently, I could at least paint and put a brave face on it . . . I'm going to go out until I've found a place and a house that suit me," Claude Monet wrote to a friend in 1883. "Once I get properly installed, I shall come to Paris only once a month . . . ."

Uninspired by the suburban town of Poissy, where he had lived for two years in a rented house with his two young sons, his companion, Alice Hoschedé, and her six children, Monet was anxious for a fresh start. At forty-two, he found himself the head of a large household with ten mouths to feed, in addition to the servants he employed even when he couldn't afford it. Still struggling to make a living from his paintings, he needed stability.

So the stout, black-bearded artist set out to explore the small villages of the Seine River valley in the countryside around Paris, in search of a new, more sympathetic, home. Monet had been captivated by water since his childhood on the Normandy coast, where he began painting landscapes as a teenager. His various residences outside Paris–at Bougival, Argenteuil, Vétheuil, and Poissy–were all situated along the serpentine course of the Seine, which he painted in all its shifting moods and seasons.

Travelling by train toward Normandy, Monet discovered Giverny, a small farming village about fifty miles northwest of Paris. Nestled among the hills on the east bank of the Seine at the junction of the Epte River, Giverny overlooked wheat fields and meadows stippled with willows, poplars, wild iris, and poppies. The town was almost medieval in appearance, with its half-timbered houses and barns. Monet was instantly enchanted. "I am in ecstasy. Giverny is splendid country for me," he exclaimed.

In 1883, he rented a long, pink, stucco house with a

Undiminished to this day, the beauty of Monet's property at Giverny, including the lily pond (opposite), was an Impressionist's dream come true.

flowering orchard. Situated on a slope between the high village road, today called rue Claude Monet, and the Chemin du Roy, the main road between Vernon and Gasny that ran alongside a small railway, the two-acre property was known as Le Pressoir, the former site of a cider press, a common feature of this region renowned for its apple orchards, cider, and Calvados.

Over the years, Monet made several alterations to his home, converting the old barn on the west wing into a parlor and a studio and expanding and modernizing the kitchen on the east wing. The main house, now carefully restored to its original appearance, remained largely unchanged, with four rooms on both the first and the second floors, an attic, and a cellar. The pink stucco façade is still covered with ivy, its brilliant green echoed in the shutters, doors, and veranda, where Monet liked to relax after dinner. His friend and dealer Paul Durand-Ruel paid for the move, and his continued financial support enabled the large family to live here comfortably.

No sooner had Monet settled in than he began reworking the small garden and orchard in front of his house so that there would always be flowers to paint. He drew endless inspiration from the irises, poppies, daisies, gladioli, roses, dahlias, and wisteria, and the Japanese cherry, apple, willow, and yew trees that envelop Giverny in a profusion of changing colors. The sprawling garden, planted in a symmetrical layout, is divided by paths, with the Grande Allée framed by rose trellises and nasturtiums. Monet designed every aspect of this consuming work-in-progress, which he hailed as "my most beautiful masterpiece," orchestrating its hues and textures, harmonies and contrasts into a painterly tableau that would be vividly transcribed onto canvas.

Here in the Clos Normand, the orchard that gradually became Monet's garden, the artist stood at his easel, wearing his soft felt hat and wooden clogs and capturing the shifting effects of light and color at various times of day. "I am good for nothing except painting and gardening," Monet often said, asserting that he would have been a botanist had he not become a painter.

Rising before dawn so that he would benefit from the maximum amount of daylight, Monet ate a breakfast of

roasted meat, cheese, bread, butter and marmalade, a cup of chocolate, tea, and a glass of milk in the yellow dining room.

Here in this large light-infused room, Monet and Alice, who were married in 1892, also dined with family and friends. Connoisseurs of fine food and wine, they delighted in indulging guests with their hospitality. Gustave Caillebotte, Paul Cézanne, Auguste Renoir, Camille Pissarro, Alfred Sisley, the French Prime Minister Georges Clemenceau, and the poet Stéphane Mallarmé, among others, enjoyed three-course meals prepared by the family cook. Regional dishes featured local game, fish, and produce from Monet's kitchen garden at the other end of the village. Poultry was raised in his henyard near the house. Monet's appetites extended beyond the table to the forty cigarettes he purportedly smoked every day.

The large dining table, rush-seated chairs, and the pair of yellow cabinets, which contain the family's blue and white china, are typical of Norman furniture from the period. Atop the mantelpiece, inlaid with blue and white Rouen tiles, are green ceramic vases from the south of France that Monet

"This house, though modest, is nonetheless sumptuous on account of its interior and the garden . . . . The man who has conceived and established this small, familiar, magnificent world of his own is not only a great artist in the creation of his paintings, but also in the environment he has made for himself, for his own delight. This house and garden are likewise a work of art, and Monet has invested his life in the creating and perfecting of it," wrote Monet's friend, the art critic Gustave Geffroy, in 1922.

The yellow dining room (opposite) is adjacent to the blue-tiled kitchen where a large steel stove and gleaming copper pots bring to mind the cook and her kitchen maids rushing to satisfy Monet's demand for punctual meals. The menus were planned by Alice Monet, an accomplished housekeeper whose upper-middle-class roots brought a certain stability and respectability to the household.

picked up on one of his painting excursions. Enlivening the walls are Japanese woodblock prints from the artist's considerable collection, which is displayed throughout the house.

Several examples adorn the blue-painted entrance hall and the blue salon, a small reading room opposite the dining room where the Monet family often read, listened to music, and played card games. Alice liked to sew here, while enjoying the company of her daughters and grandchildren. Furnished with simple, lightweight furniture, this room also functioned as a library for Monet. His books on botany, gardening, and art are stored in traditional Norman cabinets identical to those in the dining room.

The épicerie, adjacent to the blue salon, served as a storage room for dry goods and spices from around the world, which were kept in a bamboo-style sideboard along with linen tablecloths and fringed napkins. The earthenware jars and glass bottles on top contained olive oil and preserved fruits and vegetables. The épicerie also doubled as a cloakroom with its own separate entrance, so that Monet could conduct visitors directly into his studio or up the private staircase leading to his art-adorned bedroom. The bamboo

hat stand, another Asian-inspired accent that recalls Monet's
fascination with the Far East, once held the family's straw
hats, caps, and umbrellas.

From here, a few steps lead down into Monet's spacious
studio drawing room, where he both worked and entertained.
Guests were invited here after lunch to view their host's work
over coffee. The room's simple furnishings include wicker
armchairs and tables, a sofa, daybed, and two desks where
Monet drafted plans for his garden and penned many of
the more than two thousand letters he left after his death.
Although he spent most of his time painting outdoors in
every kind of weather, he brought his work back to the
studio drawing room to add finishing touches and contem-
plate his progress.

Monet spent his early years at Giverny painting views of
the surrounding countryside and the Seine, the subject of so
many previous landscapes. He would set off early in the
morning with several blank canvases, moving from one subject to another throughout the day. He often painted from his
floating studio, a rowboat that he had used at Argenteuil and
Vétheuil. It was moored at a boathouse he had built on the

Île-aux-Orties (Nettle Island), at the mouth of the Epte River.

The obsessive artist was often dissatisfied with his efforts, and at times became ill-tempered, usually because of a failed painting or a change in the weather that interrupted his progress. During these periods, his family tiptoed around him in respectful silence. Sometimes he grew so depressed that he stayed in his room all day or spent the night at a hotel in the nearby town of Vernon. But when his work went well, he was cheerful and approachable.

By the late 1880s, in an effort to better capture the effects of changing light, Monet began to focus on series paintings —interdependent images of the same motif captured at different times of day and in varying weather conditions and seasons. Rather than wait for a specific light effect to return so that he could finish one canvas, he worked on several at once.

Monet claimed that his first true series was of the haystacks. One day near the house, the light changed, and in a moment of inspiration he asked Blanche Hoschedé, a painter herself who often accompanied her stepfather on his expeditions, to bring him another canvas. He repeated the request several times that day. Soon, the artist adopted this impulse as his customary method of working, explaining, " . . . the further I move ahead, the more I realize that I must work very hard to achieve what I'm looking for: 'instanta-neousness,' especially the envelope, the same evenly suffused light everywhere."

Upstairs, above the studio, Monet's bedroom is a haven of airy calm, illuminated by late afternoon light, with a view of the garden. This spare, elegant room is furnished with antiques that the artist bought when the wealth of his later years allowed him to indulge his passion for beautiful things. Prize pieces include a Louis XV bronze-mounted chest, var-nished to imitate Asian lacquerwork, and an exquisitely inlaid roll-top desk, whose design approaches the more restrained Louis XVI style reflected in the white marble fireplace.

His collection of works by Cézanne, Manet, Renoir, and other contemporaries that once enlivened these quarters has been dispersed to museums throughout the world. The paintings now hanging on the cloth-covered walls include

Monet's bedroom (opposite) overlooks the garden at Giverny. His neoclassical bed was once outfitted with lace pillowcases and linen sheets embroidered with his initials.

The paintings of Monet that originally hung in the studio drawing room have since been replaced with replicas. Colorful kilims covered the hardwood floors. Displayed throughout the room today are family photographs, including an image of Monet by Nadar that captures the penetrating gaze of the aging artist.

those by the American Impressionists Lilla Cabot Perry, Theodore Butler (the husband of Monet's stepdaughter, Suzanne), and Monet's stepdaughter, Blanche, who also became his daughter-in-law when she married his son, Jean.

Adjoining Monet's bedroom was his dressing room, which was furnished with a mirror, a marble-topped wash-stand, and an armoire where he kept his clothes. Always a stylish dresser, even during the impoverished days of his youth, Monet usually wore tweed, wool, or cotton-and-linen jackets buttoned only at the top, a vest, wide pants, shirts with lacy cuffs, and a soft felt or straw hat. Paris tailors pro-vided him with outfits for both city and country. In Alice's dressing room next door, a marble-topped dresser once held her tortoiseshell combs and silver-lidded glass bottles and jars containing cosmetics and floral perfumes. Candles sufficed for light until electricity came to the house in 1909. Alice's adjoining bedroom is adorned with simple pine furni-ture in the neoclassical style and a black marble fireplace with a blue-framed mirror. The Japanese prints displayed on the walls depict graceful courtesans and women engaged in domestic activities. From here, Alice had access to the children's rooms on the other side of the staircase.

Alice's bright, intimate bedroom was her refuge from the demands of running a large household. Surrounded by family photographs and other personal mementos, she kept a diary and wrote letters at a small table near the window overlooking the garden, keeping her husband apprised of daily events at Giverny when he was travelling. Her sophisticated taste was expressed in dresses designed by Charles Worth, cashmere shawls, and a collection of decorative watchcases engraved with her initials.

Monet had come a long way from his years of struggle to the refined life he enjoyed at Giverny. By the end of the nineteenth century, his reputation was established. Critical and popular opinion had turned in his favor. His paintings were selling for considerable sums—as much as 40 to 50 thousand francs at his death. In 1890, after renting for seven years, he bought the house at Giverny for 22 thousand francs, building a second studio several years later to accommodate his larger-scale works. The staff of the Claude Monet Foundation now work and live in this building, which also provided additional living space for the Monet family. Monet also built three greenhouses where he cultivated exotic ferns and orchids.

By the turn of the century, the tens of thousands of flowers in Monet's gardens required the attention of six gardeners. Wynford Dewhurst, author of *Impressionist Painting* (1904) observed: "Monet is seen in his most genial moods when, with cigar for company, he strolls through his propriété at Giverny, discussing the grafting of plants and other agricultural mysteries with his numerous blue-bloused and sabotted gardeners . . . In his domain at Giverny . . . each season of the year brings its appointed and distinguishing colour scheme. Nowhere else can be found such a prodigal display of rare and marvelously beautiful colour effects, arranged from flowering plants . . . from every quarter of the globe."

In 1893, Monet bought a tract of land on the other side of the Chemin du Roy, beyond the railway. With permission from the local authorities, he diverted a tributary of the Epte

Claude Monet: *The Boat in Giverny*
(c. 1887), Musée d'Orsay, Paris;
Giraudon/Art Resource, New York.

River into a pond to create an exquisite water garden that he
surrounded with poplars, weeping willows, roses, irises, rhodo-
dendrons, azaleas, Japanese peonies, and bamboo groves.
Inspired by Japanese prints, Monet also built an arched green
bridge across the pond. Bedecked with hanging mauve and
white wisteria, the bridge appears in a series of paintings from
1899–1900. Monet took up this subject again in the early 1920s
in boldly painted works which approach abstraction.

Unlike the symmetrical Clos Normand, the water garden
is Japanese in style. Accessible via an underpass linking it to
the main flower garden, the pond still glistens with the exotic
water lilies that appear, beginning in the late 1890s, in the
paintings Monet called *Nymphéas*, after the scientific name
for a white variety of water lily. Marcel Proust described the
pond in 1913 in *Remembrance of Things Past*: "Here and there,
on the surface, there floated, blushing like a strawberry, the
scarlet heart of a lily set in a ring of white petals."

Above all, this garden inspired Monet's mystical relationship with nature. "He would remain here in his armchair for hours without moving, without speaking, peering at the undersides of passing, sunlit things, trying to read in their reflections the elusive glimmer where mysteries are revealed," observed his close friend Clemenceau.

"I want to paint the air in which the bridge, the house and the boat lie," Monet proclaimed. "The beauty of the air in which they are, and that is nothing other than impossible." Monet set up easels around the pond so that he could work from different perspectives at different hours of the day. After enlarging the pond in 1901, he painted a suite of forty-eight canvases that were exhibited to great critical acclaim. After 1904, the landscape surrounding the pond gradually disappeared from the canvases as his paintings became increasingly abstract.

"The effect varies unceasingly. Not only from one season to another but from one minute to the next, because the water lilies are far from being the only thing in the show," observed Monet. "The essence of the motif is the mirror of water whose appearance is constantly being modified by the patches of sky reflected in it which imbue it with life and movement. The passing cloud, the cooling breeze . . . the wind that stirs and suddenly blows with full force, the light that fades and is reborn are all things . . . that transfigure the color and shape of the bodies of water."

For many years, he had envisioned creating a continuous circular band of paintings of the pond that would envelop viewers in an environment of beauty and serenity as sublime as nature itself. Encouraged by Clemenceau, he began working on the Grandes Decorations in 1914, a project that occupied him for the rest of his life. He also constructed a third studio large enough to contain these monumental *Nymphéas* canvases. Completed in 1916, the concrete and glass, sky-lit water lily studio is now decorated with reproductions of Monet's works, along with enlarged photographs of the artist, his family, and friends. In Monet's time, there were large rolling easels, a few chairs and tables, and two couches at the center, from which he and his guests viewed his work.

During this period, Monet, now in his seventies, was

lonely, depressed, nearly blind, and often discouraged with his work. Alice had died in 1911, and his eldest son, Jean, three years later. The terrible suffering and loss caused by the war compounded Monet's personal grief. In a gesture of patriotism, he supplied vegetables from his garden to a local hospital for the wounded and donated his art to public causes.

During his last years, Monet rarely left the property. Continuing to paint in his gardens and in the water lily studio, he reworked some canvases and burned others that he considered inferior. Throughout 1926, Monet's health deteriorated until his death from an incurable pulmonary illness on December 5 at the age of eighty-six. A secular ceremony was attended by local villagers, artists, journalists, dealers, and the loyal Clemenceau, who was with him during his last moments. He was buried in the family plot behind the village church, overlooking the luminous landscape of his beloved Giverny.

Giverny

Giverny is about 50 miles northwest of Paris. The small village has retained its rustic ambiance and is populated today by only 500 residents, who seem little distracted by the 500,000 visitors who flock to Giverny each year.

⚜ How To Get There

By Car

From Paris, take autoroute A-13, travelling northwest. Exit at either Vernon or Bonnières and follow the signs to Giverny. The trip takes about an hour.

By Train

Tel: (33) 08 36 35 35 39
Trains depart daily from Paris's Gare Saint-Lazare (the subject of several paintings by Monet) to Vernon, a small town about two miles from Giverny. The ride on the Rouen line through the French countryside to Vernon takes from 45 to 55 minutes, depending upon the time and day. There are different schedules for weekdays and weekends. Round trip fare is 134 francs. Tickets should be purchased at the windows marked Grandes Lignes. Before boarding, don't forget to validate (*composter*) your ticket at the orange post-like structures located throughout the train stations (often near the tracks). Failure to do so will result in a fine from train inspectors on board. Trains leave frequently, some just minutes apart. If you are early to the station, do not assume that the train waiting at your designated platform is leaving for your destination. Board as closely as possible to departure time.

Taxis

Tel: (33) 02 32 21 31 31
Upon arrival in Vernon, take one of the numerous taxis waiting at the station to Giverny. One-way fare ranges from 55 francs (day) to 75 francs (evening).

Buses

Tel: (33) 02 32 71 06 39
Buses to Giverny also depart from the station, but because bus schedules don't always coordinate with train schedules, a taxi is recommended. The ten-minute bus ride is about 19 francs one way.

Bicycle Rentals

If you prefer a more leisurely trip, rent a bicycle at the Vernon train station (55 francs per day, 1000 francs deposit) or across the street at the Cafe Les Amis de Monet (80 francs per day; 50 francs per half-day).

Horse-drawn Wagons

Tel: (33) 02 32 51 35 13
Another option is to take a horse-drawn wagon (40 francs round-trip), which makes several trips per day between Vernon and Giverny.

⚜ House and Studio of Claude Monet

Claude Monet Foundation

27620 Giverny
Tel: (33) 02 32 51 28 21
Fax: (33) 02 32 51 54 18
Claude Monet's son, Michel, bequeathed the painter's home and gardens to the Académie des Beaux-Arts in 1966. After a large-scale restoration, and aided by considerable financial support from American individuals and foundations, the Claude Monet Foundation, comprising Monet's house and studio, opened to the public in 1980.
HOURS: Open every day but Monday, from April 1 to November 1, 10 a.m. to 6 p.m. If you desire a specialized tour, write to the Foundation for a list of guides who operate independently. Groups should make a reservation in advance.
ENTRY FEE: 35 francs; 25 francs per person for groups and those under 18.

Les Nymphéas

Tel: (33) 02 32 21 20 31
This small restaurant and tea salon, named after the title of Monet's celebrated water lily paintings, is located on rue Claude Monet near the parking area behind Monet's house. This is a lovely place to stop for lunch after a morning visit to Monet's property. Meals can be taken indoors in a cafe setting or on an outdoor terrace. Light fare includes salads, quiche, and desserts.
HOURS: Open every day but Monday from April through October.

Other Foundation Services

A seed and flower shop adjacent to Les Nymphéas restaurant offers a selection of gift items. Another gift shop, located inside the cavernous water lily studio adjacent to Monet's home, sells an extensive array of Monet-related souvenirs, including postcards, posters, t-shirts, jewelry, and paints, as well as reproductions of Monet's garden tools and clothing. The Monet Foundation also maintains three apartments and a large studio for use by American artists.

♧ Giverny Sites

American Museum
99, rue Claude Monet
27620 Giverny
Tel: (33) 02 32 51 94 65
Located just steps away from Monet's home and gardens, The American Museum was founded in 1992 by the American businessman and art collector, Daniel J. Terra, and his wife, Judith, owners of the Terra Museum of American Art in Chicago. Home to one of the largest collections of American Impressionist paintings in the world, the museum pays homage to the hundreds of American painters who came to Giverny at the turn of the century to work in the presence of the French master. On display here are works by Mary Cassatt, John Singer Sargent, Theodore Robinson, William Metcalf, Frederick MacMonnies, Lilla Cabot Perry, Theodore Butler, Frederick Frieseke, and others, many of which emphasize the historical connection between American and French art. One of the highlights of the collection is Theodore Robinson's *The Wedding March*, which documents the procession through Giverny at the wedding of the American painter Theodore Butler and Monet's stepdaughter, Suzanne Hoschedé. Temporary exhibitions showcase contemporary art from the Americas. Surrounded by colorful gardens that augment those of Monet, the museum is housed in an unobtrusive building that blends into the countryside. A small gift shop and restaurant complete the complex.

The menu at the museum's restaurant, Les Saisons de Giverny, includes salads, pasta, roasted salmon, cheeseburgers, and desserts, which can be enjoyed on a charming, ivy-covered terrace.

The museum also offers free art classes during the summer. Participants can paint in the muse-um gardens or among the poppies and lavender in the surrounding fields with easels and materials provided by the museum.

HOURS: Open every day except Monday from April 1 to November 1, 10 a.m. to 6 p.m. (the same hours as Monet's house and gardens). Telephone for group reservations.

House of Lilla Cabot Perry
Corner of rue du Pressoir and rue Claude Monet
The Boston artist Lilla Cabot Perry's house and garden, Le Hameau, is not far from the American Museum. Barely visible behind a stone wall, it is now the site of four studios, restored by the Terra Foundation for use by artists. Perry's house is also used for art-related receptions and seminars. Perry spent summers painting in Giverny at the turn of the century. She received gardening and painting advice from her neighbor, Monet.

House of Frederick and Mary Fairchild MacMonnies
34, rue Claude Monet
The American sculptor Frederick MacMonnies and his wife, the painter Mary Fairchild MacMonnies, lived in an old priory named Le Moutier, which the couple's friends called MacMonastery. Its half-timbered stucco façade and sloping red-tile roof are typical of the medieval architecture that recalls Giverny's earliest days.

House of Mary Cassatt
7, rue du Colombier
Mary Cassatt, a contemporary of Monet and the most celebrated of the artists who formed the American colony at Giverny, lived in this tall pink house. Cassatt, noted for her intimate portraits of mothers and children, was one of the most ardent promoters of French Impressionism in America.

Saint-Radegonde Church and Cemetery
Rue Claude Monet
The Romanesque Saint-Radegonde Church is located in the medieval quarter of the village. Monet is buried in the family grave in the adjoining cemetery. Now overgrown with vegetation, it is located at the beginning of the hillside, to the immediate right of the church as you approach from the street. The hill behind the church is a good place for a panoramic view of Giverny, its flowering orchards and broad fields enveloped in the magical light and color that so captivated Monet and the American painters who flocked here from the late 1880s to the outbreak of World War I. The American painter Theodore Butler married Monet's stepdaughter, Suzanne Hoschedé, in this church in 1892; the wedding is depicted in Theodore Robinson's painting, *The Wedding March*, on display at the American Museum.

Hôtel Baudy
81, rue Claude Monet
27620 Giverny
Tel: (33) 02 32 21 10 03
Hôtel Baudy was the inn and meeting place of the French and American Impressionists from 1887 to 1914. Operated by Lucien and Angelina Baudy, it began as a cafe and grocery store. Its pink exterior and green shutters are reminiscent of Monet's house, just down the road on rue Claude Monet. Mary Cassatt, John Singer Sargent, Theodore Butler, William Metcalf, Theodore Robinson, Lilla Cabot Perry, Cézanne, Renoir, and Rodin all ate and drank here, some staying for weeks at a time. Paintings by many of the Americans who worked in Giverny still animate the walls.

Hôtel Baudy was noted for its modest, well-kept rooms and excellent food, and for the hospitality of its owners. Madame Baudy treated the artists like members of her fami-

ly, allowed them to leave paintings in exchange for payment, and cooked their favorite dishes. To further accommodate their guests, the Baudys built a studio in the rose garden at the rear of their hotel. Now a small museum, the studio is still filled with paint brushes, palettes, easels, paint tubes, and plaster casts that give it the appearance of having just been used. Hôtel Baudy was also the site of lively evening activity. The boarders gathered in the dining room to play pool or chess, or to listen to piano music. There were dances and costume parties, too.

Monet visited periodically. Constantly disrupted by American artists knocking at his door for advice, he was particularly protective of his stepdaughters. He forced Blanche Hoschedé to end her romance with the young American painter John Breck, one of the founders of the American colony at Giverny, and an outspoken advocate of the charms of the village —much to Monet's dismay.

The old hotel now functions as a restaurant serving salads, sandwiches, omelets, vegetable platters, smoked salmon, and other dishes. There is dining both inside and outside in the garden for individuals and large groups.

HOURS: Studio open every day but Monday from April 1 to October 31, 10 a.m. to 6 p.m. Restaurant open from 11 a.m. to 9:30 p.m. Closed Sunday night and Monday.

Art Study Giverny

4, rue Blanche Hoschedé Monet
27620 Giverny
Tel: (33) 02 32 51 98 67
OR CONTACT
5724 Flamingo Dr.
Cape Coral, FL 33904
Tel: (941) 542-4166
Art Study Giverny, founded by American artist Gale Bennett and Canadian artist Janice Proctor, who teach painting here, offers English-speaking artists the opportunity to study and paint in Monet's gardens and around Giverny. Instruction is available in all media and tailored to individual needs. Twelve-day sessions, from April through October, are limited to eight students per

The American and French Impressionists who came to Giverny at the turn of the 20th century often worked in this studio at Hôtel Baudy.

La Grande Allée leads through Monet's magnificent gardens to his sprawling pink stucco house.

session. The $2,100 fee includes art instruction; museum fees in Giverny, Auvers-sur-Oise, and Versailles; permission to paint in Monet's gardens; painting and sightseeing trips around Southern Normandy; and transportation to and from Charles de Gaulle airport in Paris. Also included are gourmet meals and lodging one block from Monet's garden in a Norman-style lodge with beamed ceilings and a fireplace. Rooms are furnished in a turn-of-the-century style similar to Monet's house.

♣ Dining

(In addition to the above-mentioned restaurants affiliated with the Monet Foundation, American Museum, and Hotel Baudy)

Les Jardins de Giverny
Chemin du Roy
27620 Giverny
Tel: (33) 02 32 21 60 80
Fax: (33) 02 32 51 93 77

Situated along the main road separating Monet's house from his lily pond, this large Norman-style stone house dates from 1912. Monet, Clemenceau, and other notables ate here in the elegant dining room overlooking a garden filled with exotic banana plants, bamboo, and gingko trees. During Monet's time, this restaurant was a private residence whose owners loved to entertain. Today, meals are also served in a small sunroom and on the garden terrace. Menus ranging from 130 to 230 francs include homemade foie gras, smoked salmon, grilled bass, lobster salad, roast chicken with cider sauce, and grilled leg of duck in mustard sauce, among other dishes made from fresh, local products. HOURS: Open during the summer months from 12 p.m. to 3 p.m.; during the winter months (except February) from 12 p.m. to 2 p.m. Dinner served Saturday night only from 7:30 p.m. to 9 p.m. Closed Monday.

L'Auberge du Vieux Moulin
21, rue de la Falaise
27620 Giverny
Tel: (33) 02 32 51 46 15
Fax: (33) 02 32 51 63 90
Situated across the street from the old mill for which it is named, this former inn has an appealing dining room with stucco walls and a stone fireplace. Complete with indoor and outdoor terrace dining, L'Auberge serves traditional French cuisine with menus ranging from 125 francs to 270 francs. Dishes include patés, duck terrine, filet of beef, lamb, tuna steak, salmon with champagne sauce, and apple and pear tarts. Large reception rooms accommodate groups of up to 180 people; there is even Saturday night dancing.
HOURS: Open for lunch and dinner every day but Sunday night and Monday.

La Grenouillère
Rue de la Falaise
27620 Giverny
Tel: (33) 02 32 51 23 59
Named after the resort and floating cafe along the Seine outside Paris that was patronized by the Impressionists and immortalized in Monet's and Renoir's paintings, this charming outdoor cafe is situated in the woods along an Epte River tributary. It is just across the street from L'Auberge du Vieux Moulin. Quick fare such as salads, omelets, french fries, pastries, ice cream, and cold drinks are served.
HOURS: Open from 12 p.m. to 5 p.m. every day.

La Bonne Étable
9, rue de la Falaise
27620 Giverny
Tel: (33) 02 32 51 66 32
A few feet away from L'Auberge du Vieux Moulin on the same side of the street, this cozy brasserie occupies an old Norman-style stone house with a fireplace. Menus from 75 francs to 135 francs include salads, sandwiches, omelets, beef, duck, seafood, and homemade pastries.
HOURS: Open April through October every day but Monday for lunch, 12:30 p.m. to 3 p.m; dinner Saturday night only, 7:30 p.m. to 10:30 p.m.

La Terrasse
87, rue Claude Monet
27620 Giverny
Tel: (33) 02 32 51 36 09
Steps away from the Hôtel Baudy, this intimate cafe and tea salon is one of the best places in Giverny to stop for a quick bite. Furnished with a few old tables, La Terrasse offers tasty salads and cheese and cold cut platters for 40 to 50 francs. Regional products such as Calvados, cider, Camembert, foie gras, patés, pastries, wines, and homemade jams are also for sale here.
HOURS: Open April through October every day but Monday from 11 a.m. to 8 p.m.

☙ Nearby Dining

Le Verger de Giverny
1, rue Saint-Geneviève
La Chapelle Saint-Ouen
27620 Bois-Jérôme
Tel: (33) 02 32 51 29 36 OR
    (33) 02 32 51 17 44
This cider farm in the neighboring village of Bois-Jérôme is located about two miles from Monet's home. It offers cider and apple tart tastings.
HOURS: Open April through October from 12 p.m. to 7 p.m. Closed Monday and Tuesday.

Le Moulin de Fourges
38, rue du Moulin
27630 Fourges
Tel: (33) 02 32 52 12 12
Fax: (33) 02 32 52 92 56
This beautiful restaurant, situated in a rustic old water mill in the Epte valley about four miles from Giverny, is a bit further afield but well worth the visit for both its ambience and excellent meals.

Menus ranging from 130 francs to 250 francs include roast chicken, lamb, trout, salmon, filet of beef, and other dishes made in a traditional French manner. Both indoor and outdoor dining; equipped for large groups.
HOURS: Open for lunch 12 p.m. to 2 p.m.; dinner 7 p.m. to 10 p.m. Closed Sunday night and Monday.

☙ Accommodations

La Musardiere
123, rue Claude Monet
27620 Giverny
Tel: (33) 02 32 21 03 18
Not far from Monet's home, this agreeable two-star hotel is situated in a large, century-old home with a pink stucco façade. There are ten modest rooms with eclectic vintage furnishings. Price ranges are 300 francs (with shower); 320 to 400 francs (with full bath); and 420 to 470 francs (for triples). The hotel restaurant offers beef, salmon, duck, salads, omelets, soups, and quiches at à la carte prices ranging from 18 to 120 francs. There is also an adjoining crèperie with an outdoor terrace.

La Réserve
Didier and Marie Lorraine Brunet
27620 Giverny
Tel/Fax: (33) 02 32 21 99 09
Mobile: (33) 06 11 25 37 44
http://www.giverny.org/hotels/brunet
The most luxurious accommodation in Giverny, this bed-and-breakfast family residence is situated in a large, old-world farmhouse with spacious, antique-decorated rooms, wood-beamed ceilings, and modern conveniences. Surrounded by woods and orchards in a beautiful natural setting, it is the perfect country getaway. Five bedrooms with private bathrooms range from 450 to 650 francs, breakfast included. Bikes, billiards, pedestrian tours, and drawing and painting equip-

Monet is buried in the cemetery of Saint Radegonde Church in the medieval quarter of Giverny.

ment are available to guests. Several golf courses are nearby. A car or taxi will be necessary to reach this secluded location just a few miles from Monet's home.

HOURS: Open April 1 to November 1. Also available in winter by reservation only.

Chambres d'Hôtes

Marie-Claire Boscher
Rue du Colombier
27620 Giverny
Tel: (33) 02 32 51 39 70
Located off rue Claude Monet in the center of the village, this bed-and-breakfast was a popular cafe and restaurant during the 1920s. There are three recently renovated rooms with simple, tasteful furnishings. One room has a balcony overlooking the garden, complete with crowing roosters. Prices range from 260 to 350 francs, breakfast included; 100 francs supplement for three people.

Chambres D'Hôtes Giverny

Eric and Christelle Carrière
6, rue aux Juifs
27620 Giverny
Tel: (33) 02 32 51 02 96
This charming bed-and-breakfast is located in the medieval quarter (near the church) on the oldest street in Giverny–Street of the Jews–which is lined with several preserved half-timbered houses and a walled medieval monastery (now privately owned). Late medieval stone houses can also be found on nearby rue des Chandeliers. The accommodations occupy a 300-year-old house with four rustic rooms and modern bathrooms. One room is situated in an adjacent smaller building that is equipped with its own small kitchen and bathroom. Prices for individual rooms range from 260 francs to 300 francs, breakfast included. The small house can be rented for 350 francs per night or 2,000 francs per week.

✤ Nearby Accommodations

Château de Brécourt

27120 Pacy-sur-Eure Douains
Tel: (33) 02 32 52 40 50/32 52 41 39
Fax: (33) 02 32 52 69 65
This four-star hotel is situated
about nine miles from Giverny in
a beautiful Louis XIII-style castle
surrounded by moats and a
sprawling wooded park. There are
30 elegantly appointed rooms, two
dining rooms, a tennis court, and
swimming pool. Prices range from
410 to 1,425 francs. Accommodations
are available for large groups.

Hôtel Normandy

1, avenue Pierre-Mendes-France
27200 Vernon
Tel: (33) 02 32 51 97 97
Fax: (33) 02 32 21 01 66
Located five minutes from the train
station in Vernon, this three-star
hotel has 47 rooms and three suites,
each with bathrooms and modern
conveniences (toilets separate). The
building is old, but rooms are decorated in a clean, contemporary style.
The hotel has its own bar and
restaurant. Prices range from 310
to 320 francs (for a street view).
Breakfast is extra at 40 francs
per person.

✤ Short Excursions

Vernon

Given its proximity to Giverny, the
small Norman town of Vernon,
with its 15th-century half-timbered
houses, is worth a quick visit.

Musée de Vernon

12, rue du Pont
Tel.: (33) 02 32 21 28 09
The main attraction in Vernon for
art lovers, the museum's collection is
housed in a 16th- to 18th-century
mansion and includes two paintings
by Monet (one is a 1908 *Nymphéas*)
and works by other Giverny artists
such as Blanche Hoschedé (Monet's

stepdaughter), Theodore Butler, and
Frederick and Mary Fairchild
MacMonnies. Also on display are
works by the Nabis painters Pierre
Bonnard, Édouard Vuillard, and
Maurice Denis (all of whom knew
and visited Monet), as well as a
medieval statue collection and arche-
ological relics found near Vernon.

Vernon Tourist Office

36, rue Carnot
Tel: (33) 02 32 51 39 60

Rouen

Monet disciples may want to make
the longer trip to the picturesque
city of Rouen, the capital of the
Norman empire from the tenth
through twelfth centuries. Many
of its medieval half-timbered houses
are still standing. Just over an hour's
train ride from Paris's Gare Saint-
Lazare, Rouen is the fourth stop
after Vernon. Although its claim to
fame rests on the tragic fate of Joan
of Arc, who was burned at the stake
here in 1431 in the place du Vieux
Marché, Rouen is also the site of
the Gothic Notre Dame Cathedral,
which Monet captured in a series of
paintings from 1892 to 1894. He set
his easel opposite the west façade of
the cathedral, painting more than
twenty versions under varying light
and atmospheric conditions, com-
plaining in letters to his wife about
the difficulty of the task.

Rouen's Fine Arts Museum displays
works by Monet, Renoir, Sisley, and
other European masters from the
16th through 20th centuries.

This city is also the birthplace of
French author Gustave Flaubert,
and the setting for his scandalous
1857 novel, *Madame Bovary*. The
Flaubert Museum, in the building
where he grew up, houses some of
his possessions. Flaubert fans may
also want to visit his estate in nearby Croisset. Call the Rouen tourist
office for information.

Rouen Tourist Office

25, place de la Cathédrale
Tel: (33) 02 32 08 32 40

Club Hôtelier Rouennais

(24-hour accommodation service)
Tel: (33) 02 35 71 76 77

Museums in Paris with works by Monet:

✤ Musée D'Orsay
✤ Musée Marmottan
✤ Musée de L'Orangerie

Charles-François Daubigny: *Boats
on the Oise* (1865), Musée d'Orsay,
Paris; photo © J. Schorman,
Réunion des Musées Nationaux/Art
Resource, New York.

Charles-François Daubigny

One of the first artists to work entirely out of doors, Charles-François Daubigny depicted the beauty of the French countryside in its diverse aspects and moods, particularly its shimmering rivers, ponds, and sea views. Born in 1817 in Paris into a family of artists, he spent his childhood in the village of Valmondois, north of Paris. Here, not far from his future home in Auvers-sur-Oise, Daubigny's lifelong love of the rural landscape was awakened. As a young man, the artist worked as a painting restorer at the Louvre, where his drastic alterations eventually led to his dismissal. He supported his wife and children by illustrating books and magazines, but his true artistic energies were invested in the landscapes he painted for exhibition. Nomadic by temperament, Daubigny painted from the Normandy coast to the Fontainebleau forest south of Paris, where he became a member of the artists' colony at nearby Barbizon. An appreciative but conservative critic noted, "I do not know anyone who has a more intimate feeling for nature, and who can better make it felt. But why does he only produce rough sketches . . . Is M. Daubigny afraid of ruining his work by finishing it?" In order to facilitate his open-air painting and to be close to water, Daubigny purchased a boat in 1857 and converted it into a floating studio dubbed the Botin—a vernacular term for small boat. Gliding along the Marne, Seine, and Oise rivers, he painted some of his most memorable landscapes in an innovative style that prefigured Impressionism. By 1860, Daubigny had acquired a regular following of collectors enamored of his river landscapes. Improved finances allowed him to purchase property and build a home and studio in Auvers-sur-Oise. With Daubigny at its center, this small village was ultimately to attract three generations of artists: landscape painters, Impressionists, and Post-Impressionists.

Paul Nadar: *Charles-François Daubigny*, Caisse Nationale des Monuments Historiques et des Sites, Paris; © Arch. Phot. Paris/ CMN.

Daubigny in Auvers-sur-Oise 1862–1878

Forefather of Impressionism

"I have bought a property . . . in Auvers," Charles-François Daubigny wrote to his friend and first biographer, Frédéric Henriet, in August 1860. "It is covered with beans and I will plant a few legs of lamb on them if you come to see me. I am in the midst of building myself a studio, eight meters by six, surrounded by several rooms that I hope I will be able to use by next spring. Father Corot found Auvers very beautiful and pledged me to settle myself in for a part of the year."

By this time Daubigny was a successful painter. His riverside views had become so popular that he once lamented: "If only I could paint a picture that wouldn't sell!" Daubigny hoped that the small village of Auvers-sur-Oise would provide him with a haven where he could work in peace.

Situated twenty-two miles north of Paris in the countryside he had grown to love as a child, Daubigny's Villa des Vallées (House of the Valley) was completed in 1861. The property stands on a street now named for him, overlooking a beautiful garden in a quiet area off the village's main street, just steps away from the Ravoux Inn, where van Gogh would spend his final days three decades later.

Formerly surrounded by thatched-roof cottages, the wood and stucco villa, with its red shutters and high-ceilinged studio, was designed by Daubigny's friend Achille Oudinot. Oudinot, the painter Camille Corot, the caricaturist Honoré Daumier, Daubigny himself, and his son, Karl, also decorated the interior walls, a testament to the camaraderie, prodigious talent, and generosity of spirit that characterized Daubigny's life and work.

Luminous murals adorn the entry hall. There are country scenes by Daubigny alongside Karl Daubigny's seascapes of

The walls throughout the Villa des Valées (opposite) are enlivened with charming motifs from the surrounding countryside, which Daubigny had grown to love as a child.

Daubigny's home was Auvers's first gathering place for artists, and it was through his fame that the village became well known. Among the many visitors to Daubigny's house were his close friends Corot and Daumier, as well as Renoir, Morisot, Pissarro, and Cézanne.

the Normandy coast and views of his father's studio boat, the Botin, on the Oise river. A mirror has replaced Daumier's depiction of Don Quixote, which now hangs in Paris's Musée d'Orsay, home to many of Daubigny's finest works.

The gregarious artist often took his meals here in the vestibule so that he would have an optimal view of the garden. The adjacent dining room is empty but for a small wooden table and an ebony clock on the fireplace mantel. After the artist's death in 1878, most of the furniture was sold at auction, along with hundreds of paintings and drawings. The colorful panels of rabbits, birds, fish, flowers, fruits, and vegetables painted by Daubigny, his son, Karl, and his daughter, Cécile, infuse the room with a pastoral abundance reminiscent of Daubigny's paintings.

Daubigny moved his family into Villa des Vallées in 1862, and spent several months here each summer, working the rest of the year in Paris. He felt at home among the wooded valleys, hills, and plains of Auvers, which offered a stunning range of subjects to paint. He was just a few miles from his childhood home in Valmondois, where he had lived with his foster family, the Bazots, and was first introduced to the charms of the countryside. "For who, tell me, has ever been cured of his childhood?" Daubigny rhapsodized. He returned to Valmondois frequently throughout his life, often by coach or on foot from the city, describing the village as possessing "the most varied contours that I know of in the Paris region." Beginning in 1835, he spent summers there painting.

Daubigny discovered Auvers-sur-Oise around the same time, and in 1854 he began visiting regularly with Corot. A colony of landscape painters soon formed around these two masters, who were among the first to liberate themselves from the confines of academic painting and the rigid rules of the Salon. Unlike most of their contemporaries, who followed the tradition of painting Greek and Latin tableaux based on studio poses, Daubigny, Corot, and their Barbizon friends set up their easels in the forests and fields and along the riverside. They passed on to their admiring students technical discoveries relating to light, color, and composition, as well as a passion for conveying the initial impressions of landscapes painted in the open air.

Among the illustrious guests at his many parties and musical soirées—both Daubigny and Karl sang well—were his close friends Corot and Daumier, as well as the Impressionists Pierre-Auguste Renoir, Berthe Morisot —Edouard Manet's sister-in-law who lived and painted in the nearby hamlet of Chou in the 1860s and '70s—and Camille Pissarro, who lived and painted in neighboring Pontoise from 1872 to 1884 and was a mentor to many Impressionists. The Post-Impressionist Paul Cézanne, who was heavily influenced by Pissarro while living in Auvers from 1872 to 1874, was another frequent visitor.

Daubigny was also friendly with Dr. Paul-Ferdinand Gachet, the amateur artist, engraver, Impressionists' patron, and homeopathic physician who would later minister to van Gogh. His home on what is now called rue Dr. Gachet, several hundred feet from Daubigny's villa, was another gathering place for artists.

The proximity of Daubigny's residence to the homes of Gachet, Cézanne, and Pissarro encouraged frequent visits

Charles-François Daubigny:
The Studio on the Boat (c. 1857),
Musée du Louvre, Paris; Photo ©
J. G. Berizzi, Réunion des Musées
Nationaux/Art Resource, New York.

Charles-François Daubigny:
The Houseboat (c. 1857), photo
© Michele Bellot, Musée du
Louvre, Paris; Réunion des Musées
Nationaux/Art Resource, New York.

among the artists and nurtured a constant flow of inspiration and ideas. Daubigny and his artist friends also socialized at Cafe Partois (now a restaurant called Le Verre Placide) across from the Auvers train station, often over glasses of the potent, highly addictive absinthe.

Daubigny's active social life, however, did not interfere with his work. He frequently could be found on the Île de Vaux, an island in the Oise River, where he pursued many of his favorite themes. He arrived there in his Botin, which remained tied to the river bank while he painted on shore beneath a large parasol that protected him from the sun. Here, friends and students came to paint and seek his advice.

His friends also accompanied him on numerous voyages along the Oise and Seine, painting together in the small cabin studio aboard the thirty-foot, flat-bottomed Botin, which was equipped with artists' materials, cooking utensils, provisions, and lockers for bedding. Believing that it was "from the banks of the rivers that one sees the most beautiful landscapes," Daubigny delighted in capturing the fleeting effects of light on water at different times of day and under varied weather conditions.

Daubigny was dubbed "captain" of the Botin and Karl its "cabin-boy;" Corot was appointed "honorary admiral." The whole crew took part in festivals that celebrated the departure and return of the vessel, a replica of which now stands in the garden behind Villa des Vallées. Naturally playful, Daubigny recorded his amusing nautical adventures in a series of etchings, *Voyage en Bateau*.

Some of these etchings hang in Daubigny's bedroom, which now functions as an exhibition space for his works, including watercolors of the local landscape and a small painting of his wife. Also on display are a small sunset study depicted in the portrait and a pencil-and-charcoal portrait of the artist at age seven, drawn by Daubigny's uncle, Pierre.

"Like his art, Daubigny had charming candor and frankness," according to the landscape painter Jules Breton. The colorful wall paintings in his daughter Cécile's bedroom, which he undertook in celebration of her twentieth birthday, reveal his irrepressible enthusiasm and tender heart. White

In Cécile's bedroom, birds and butterfly nets, tennis racquets and toys, wreaths of flowers, and scenes from La Fontaine's fables and Perrault's fairytales merge in a wondrous pictorial universe, executed with the soft, shimmering colors and idyllic charm that pervade Daubigny's work on canvas.

lace curtains, a small antique dressing table, and a replica of Cécile's cradle underneath a pink and turquoise canopy complete this "palace of flowers," as Cécile, an artist in her own right, lovingly referred to her room.

At the urging of his friends, Daubigny extended his interior decoration to his massive, wood-paneled studio, the most impressive feature of Villa des Vallées. For seven years, beginning in 1866, Daubigny, Karl, and Oudinot spent rainy days painting three large murals that imbue the studio with a bucolic calm. Too frail to climb the ladders to paint, the elderly Corot provided charcoal sketches for the riverbank and lake scenes.

Daubigny had met Corot in 1852, beginning a long and close personal and artistic relationship. "Old Corot is a merry old soul," Daubigny wrote to a friend with affection. "I am looking forward to the mutton leg of friendship we shall be eating with him. You will see how kind he is." Noted for classical landscapes and lyrical woodland scenes, the fatherly Corot was a frequent dinner guest at Daubigny's Paris studio on the Île St. Louis, and often visited the younger artist in Auvers.

From a lofty perch beneath a soaring wood-beamed ceiling, a plaster bust of Daubigny seems to gaze calmly upon his domain, furnished with an ornately carved buffet, a Louis XV desk, a heavy oak table and chairs, and other family belongings passed down to Daubigny's great-grandson, Daniel Raskin, who has restored Villa des Vallées as closely as possible to its original 19th-century appearance.

A piano near the fireplace has replaced the original that Cécile played at her father's parties. On Corot's easel sits Karl Daubigny's last painting, a view of the garden at the villa. Karl worked beside his father in the Auvers countryside and, like his sister, showed several paintings at the Salons. But neither matched the artistic renown achieved by Daubigny.

Numerous mementos, displayed in a glass cabinet, bring Daubigny's life into closer focus. Here are the artist's pipe and tortoiseshell tobacco box, small sketches of local scenes, old tubes of paint, family photographs, Salon medals, and toys. At the Daubigny Museum in the nearby Manoir des Colombières are the artist's paint-encrusted palette, blue velvet beret, engraving plates and tools, and the Botin's green-paint-

The murals in Daubigny's studio were a collaborative effort of Daubigny, Karl, Oudinot, and Corot.

ed oars, as well as artwork by Daubigny and others who lived and worked in Auvers.

Although Daubigny used his Auvers studio to put the finishing touches on the large paintings he submitted to the Salons, he completed many works on site, whether on his Botin or in the open country. "Daubigny attached his canvas to stakes solidly planted in the ground; and there it stayed, risking the attacks of goats and bulls, and open to the pranks of naughty children," wrote his friend Henriet. "It was not taken down until it was perfectly finished. He was constantly on the alert for the right moment and ran to take up his work as soon as the weather corresponded to that of his painting."

A profound sincerity best characterizes the simple pastoral scenes for which Daubigny became known. His intuitive evocation of the spirit of place, whether distilled in the brilliance of dawn or the calm of twilight, resulted in works of eloquence and freshness.

Nonetheless, his novel technique of depicting the changing aspects of nature with light and rapid brushstrokes irritated critics such as Théophile Gautier, who in 1861 dismissed his pictures as "rough sketches" and "impressions." Although Daubigny maintained that "the best paintings are those that are unsaleable," he was still able to satisfy numerous collectors while experimenting with a freer, bolder style and shorter brushstrokes in later works.

During the last two decades of his life, the French government bought many of his pictures and made him an officer of the Legion of Honor in 1874. Despite his success, he continued his simple, itinerant life, enjoying the company of his friends at Auvers and travelling throughout Europe.

Elected to the Salon jury in 1865, Daubigny was one of the few who recognized the talents of the younger generation of painters who would later make their marks as Impressionists. Eventually, due largely to his influence, many of these painters were admitted to the Salon, much to the dismay of some officials.

In defense of Daubigny, the art critic Castagnary wrote: "If the Salon of this year is what it is, a Salon of newcomers; . . . if in this overflow of free painting, official State painting

has made a poor showing, it is all Daubigny's fault . . . Daubigny is not only a great artist, but a decent man as well. One who remembers the hardships of his own youth, and would wish to spare others the severe trials to which he himself has submitted."

Eventually accused of supporting "bad painters," Daubigny resigned from the Salon jury. In that same year, he moved his family to London to seek refuge from the Franco-Prussian War. There, he introduced Pissarro and Monet to Paul Durand-Ruel, the future Impressionist dealer who was then selling Daubigny's and Corot's works. "If I myself and several friends didn't starve to death in London, it was thanks to Daubigny," Monet later acknowledged.

By 1872, Daubigny had developed asthma and bronchitis, illnesses common to landscape artists who spent much of their time outdoors. Back in Auvers, he continued to work and travel on his Botin. After a journey on the Seine in the summer of 1877, Daubigny attended an outdoor dinner and sang under the apple trees. "We were happy to hear the melodious reverberations of his voice under this immense shelter," a friend recalled. "His voice charmed us, then filtered up to lose itself in the vast immensity. He was really at home there . . . ."

It was to be Daubigny's last summer in Auvers. He died of a heart ailment on February 19, 1878 at his home in Paris at age sixty-one. More than 1,500 people attended his funeral service, held in the church of Notre Dame de Lorette. He was buried in Paris's Père Lachaise cemetery, next to Corot, who had passed away three years earlier. Daubigny's last words were: "I am going above to see if my friend Corot has found me any subjects for landscapes."

Charles-François Daubigny: *Spring*
(c. 1857), Musée du Louvre, Paris;
Scala/Art Resource, New York.

Vincent van Gogh: *Stairway at
Auvers* (1890), The Saint Louis Art
Museum. Purchase.

Vincent Van Gogh

Impassioned painter, writer, and utopian thinker, sometime laypreacher and selfless ascetic, Vincent van Gogh created works that were revolutionary for their vibrant colors, bold brushwork, and emotional intensity. The eldest of six children, van Gogh was born in 1853 in a small Dutch village where his father was a Protestant pastor. As a child, he showed a talent for drawing, and developed his love of art while working at a gallery. Following a brief stint as an evangelist in a mining region of Belgium, van Gogh resolved to become an artist. He moved to Paris in 1886 to live with his brother Theo, his loyal financial and emotional supporter. His discovery of the Impressionists and friendships with Toulouse-Lautrec, Gauguin, and Seurat, among other noted artists, inspired him to lighten his palette and forge his distinctive modern style. Sudden fits of temper, however, caused tensions with Theo, and the exhausting pace of his work prompted a move to Arles in Provence in 1888. Rejuvenated by the rural landscape and bright light of the south, he painted with brilliant, daring color combinations and dreamed of establishing a colony of artists who would invent the painting of the future. Gauguin briefly joined him in Arles, but one of their frequent quarrels resulted in van Gogh's famous mutilation of his ear and his committal to a mental asylum. In the spring of 1890, he returned to the north of France, this time to the village of Auvers-sur-Oise, where he spent the last nine weeks of his life, producing scores of paintings in a feverish burst of creativity. Van Gogh was thirty-seven at the time of his suicide. He had painted obsessively for just ten years, and his battles with poverty, isolation, mental illness, and debilitating self-doubt soon cast him as the prototype of the tortured artist who sacrifices everything for his art. Of the nearly nine hundred paintings produced during his brief career, he had sold only one.

Vincent van Gogh: *Self-portrait* (1887), Musée d'Orsay, Paris; photo © Erich Lessing, Art Resource, New York.

Van Gogh in Auvers-sur-Oise 1890
Flame into Fire

On May 20, 1890, Vincent van Gogh boarded a train to Auvers-sur-Oise, a small, rustic village on the banks of the Oise River twenty-two miles north of Paris. The tall, broad-shouldered Dutch artist had just spent three days with his brother, Theo, and his family in Paris, where he had met his young godson, Vincent, for the first time. Van Gogh had found the city disruptive. "The noise of Paris was making such a bad impression on me that I thought it wise, for the sake of my mind, to get away from it and to go out into the country," van Gogh wrote to Paul Gauguin.

In Auvers he found a setting that was "profoundly beautiful . . . among other things, many old thatched roofs, which are getting rare," as he wrote to Theo shortly after his arrival. Today, the village still brings to mind the evocative canvases it inspired: the narrow, twisting streets fringed with linden and poplar trees; the ivy-draped stone walls and shuttered farmhouses; the courtyard gardens bathed in the green, yellow, and mauve tones of the paintings; the Romanesque church and clock tower; and the vast wheat and corn fields under the shifting clouds and swiftly changing light of the Île-de-France sky.

Van Gogh found cheap lodging across from the town hall at the small inn and cafe owned by the Ravoux family. A tiny third-floor room, which cost 3.50 francs a day, meals included, was to be his last home. Now, painstakingly restored to its original 19th-century appearance by Belgian entrepreneur Dominique-Charles Janssens, the former Cafe de la Mairie is currently known as the Ravoux Inn or House of van Gogh. It is the only one of van Gogh's thirty-eight residences that remains intact.

The cafe of the Ravoux Inn (opposite), where van Gogh stayed, has been restored to its original 19th-century appearance.

Passing through a succession of owners since van Gogh's time, the inn has a long tradition as a gathering place for artists. In 1849, the railroad put Auvers-sur-Oise less than an hour away from Paris and its Gare du Nord. Lured by the beautiful countryside that later captivated van Gogh, earlier landscape painters such as Charles-François Daubigny and Camille Corot, the Impressionists Camille Pissarro and Claude Monet, as well as Paul Cézanne and Paul Gauguin, came to Auvers to paint from nature in the open air.

As early as 1854, young artists gathered around these masters, establishing the small village as a catalyst in the evolution of French painting. The first independent Impressionist group show, organized in Paris in 1874, included many works painted in Auvers and the neighboring village of Pontoise, where Pissarro lived from 1872 to 1884. Daubigny's home and studio still stand just a few steps away from the Ravoux Inn.

It is easy to imagine van Gogh rising early for breakfast, then leaving through the back door, his canvases strapped to his back. After mornings spent painting in the village and fields, he returned for lunch, treading the black-and-white checkered tile floor to the long oak "painters' table" at the rear of the cafe. Van Gogh dined here with local artists on simple meals of meat, vegetables, salad, and bread.

In the cafe of the Ravoux Inn, green- and crimson-painted walls, a zinc bar, straw-seated chairs, and small wooden tables covered with linen tea-towels recreate the century-old ambience. A large fresco of a country scene, long covered by layers of wallpaper, has only recently been rediscovered.

After lunch, van Gogh would venture out again to paint until sunset, then return to the inn for dinner. In the evenings, he sometimes played with the Ravoux baby, Germaine, drawing for her on a slate.

"We called him family, Mr. Vincent," recalled the innkeeper's daughter, Adeline Ravoux, who described the intense lodger, as "discreet and accommodating." Although a loner, van Gogh proved to be friendly and good-natured during his stay. The artist was esteemed by the family, who were unaware of his mental frailty. It was a far different reception from that given him in Arles, in southern France,

This brown-trimmed stucco building housed a restaurant and wine merchant before being purchased in 1889 by Arthur Gustave Ravoux. He was a portly, bespectacled man with a bushy moustache who soon began renting furnished rooms to artists.

where he had lived two years earlier. There, the townsfolk had petitioned the mayor to have the "red-headed madman" institutionalized.

A modest wooden door at the top of the stairs opens into a suffocatingly small space, punctuated by a lone dormer window. This is the garret where van Gogh stayed. Here, the artist stored his canvases under his iron bed and wrote long letters by night. The small green wall cupboard held his few belongings. A straw-seated chair and table, a water jug, and a bowl for washing were the only other furnishings. In the cracks and nail holes along the barren walls where his paintings once hung to dry, his presence lingers.

Here, exhibitions of the artist's work—one painting at a time—honor his last wish: "One day or another, I believe that

I will find a way to have an exhibition of my own in a cafe," he wrote to his brother Theo.

The young Dutch painter Anton Hirschig lived in the room adjacent to van Gogh's. Now furnished with a few period antiques, the room evokes the life of an artist in Auvers at the end of the 19th century. Other painters occupied the inn's remaining rooms.

Classified a national historic monument in 1985, the inn appears the same now as when the artist moved here after a stay at the asylum at Saint-Rémy-de-Provence, where he convalesced after his falling-out with Gauguin and self-mutilation. Van Gogh's bouts of mental illness were the result of a type of epilepsy; they alternately took the form of melancho-

A narrow, winding stairway (opposite) leads to the room near the attic where van Gogh stayed. Van Gogh's garret was never used after his death because it was considered bad luck to stay in a "suicide room."

lia, hallucinations, and extreme neuroses. From the asylum, van Gogh wrote to Theo that he was "overwhelmed with boredom and grief," and anxious to return to the north to continue painting. On the advice of Pissarro, Theo arranged for his brother to be cared for in Auvers by Dr. Paul Gachet, a homeopathic physician, painter, engraver, art collector, and friend and patron of the village's Impressionists. During the last half of the nineteenth century, his home became a salon of sorts for artists such as Pissarro, Monet, Renoir, and Cézanne. Hung from floor to ceiling with paintings by his friends, the home was furnished with "black antiques, black, black, black," as van Gogh described them. Gachet, who worked in Paris, spent three days a week at Auvers with his son, Paul, and daughter, Marguerite.

Van Gogh quickly formed a friendship with the doctor, whom he found to be "rather eccentric." "I have found a true

friend in Dr. Gachet, something like another brother, so much do we resemble each other physically and also mentally," he wrote to his sister, Wilhelmina. He painted in Gachet's garden and often dined at his home, which still presides majestically at 78, rue Dr. Gachet, overlooking the Oise valley below.

His medical supervision, along with the proximity of Theo and his family, nurtured the artist's fragile mental health and encouraged his creativity. The tranquility van Gogh found in Auvers also contributed to the "aura of well-being" he felt during his first few weeks there. He plunged into his work with extraordinary speed and characteristic passion, working "to find an expression for the desperately swift passing away of things in modern life."

Van Gogh often painted the peasants of Auvers working on old farms or lingering on the roads around the Ravoux Inn. From his earliest years in Holland, he had considered himself a "peasant painter" in the tradition of Jean-François

Millet. "There is, on the face of it, nothing simpler than to paint peasants, rag men, and ordinary workmen, but nothing, no subject at all in the art of painting is as difficult as those simple characters," wrote van Gogh, who in his youth had walked about unkempt and often subsisted on crusts of bread in an effort to identify with the peasants he came to know.

The Auvers countryside provided van Gogh with an endless variety of landscapes, which he infused with the rich colors, vigorous lines, and whirling, sinuous forms that marked his paintings from the Arles and Saint-Rémy periods. He experimented with color combinations of violet and yellow, blue and orange, and techniques such as pointillist-influenced brushstrokes. His palette expanded to include the subtlest greens. But the rhythm of his Auvers canvases was more intense; they convulsed in a riot of line and color, distorting their subjects, rendering raw the vertigo of his imagination and his encroaching despair.

Van Gogh's initial sense of well-being in Auvers began to deteriorate on July 6, when he returned to the village after a day spent visiting Theo and his family in Paris. His godson had fallen ill. Theo was having financial problems with the Boussod & Valadon Gallery and had hinted that it would be difficult to continue supporting his brother.

Overwhelmed by financial worries, ignored by the public, and never satisfied with his work, van Gogh could only see himself as a failure. The painful gulf between art and life was ever-present for him. "People, they're worth more than things and as for myself, the more trouble I take with my paintings, the more painting leaves me cold. The love of art causes true love to be lost," he wrote.

He drove himself to perfection in the belief that his paintings were inferior to those of his revered masters Rembrandt, Delacroix, Millet, Corot, and Daubigny. In addition, he was tormented by fits of madness and unbearable loneliness.

During the weeks leading up to his death, van Gogh also lost confidence in Gachet, whom he believed had not taken his illness seriously. Their friendship ruptured during a violent argument. "I think we must not count on Dr. Gachet at

all," van Gogh complained to his brother. "First of all he is sicker than I am . . . . Back here, I still felt very sad and continued to feel the storm that threatens you weighing on me too. What's to be done–you see, I generally try to be fairly cheerful, but my life is also threatened at the very root, and my steps are also wavering."

Tense and exhausted, he continued to work through July of 1890. He set up his easel on the hill overlooking Auvers, painting a canvas of turbulent energy, *Wheat Field with Crows*, which would be one of his final works. The swirling spirals of his previous paintings had given way to the frenzied rhythm of short, broken lines and a distorted perspective. The figures often portrayed in his landscapes were absent. "They are immense stretches of wheat under a troubled sky, and I had no difficulty in trying to express sadness and extreme solitude," the artist wrote.

On the afternoon of July 27th, van Gogh left the Ravoux Inn after lunch, walked to a farmyard behind the Château de Léry, and shot himself in the chest. Later that evening, Monsieur Ravoux found him in his garret, curled up and bleeding on his bed. Gachet and another village doctor tended to him but found his wound inoperable. The still-lucid artist refused to respond to police questioning.

Hirschig delivered word to Theo in Paris the following day. Theo came immediately and sat by his brother's bedside day and night as van Gogh peacefully smoked his pipe. "I wish it were all over now," he lamented. In the early morning of July 29, 1890, the solitary Dutch painter died at the age of thirty-seven.

On the day of the funeral, beneath a blazing sun, Theo and about a dozen friends followed the hearse up the hill to the cemetery overlooking the wheatfield. Gachet gave the eulogy. "He was an honest man and a great artist," he said, weeping. "And there were only two things for him: humanity and art."

Of van Gogh's death, the painter Émile Bernard wrote to the poet Albert Aurier: "On the walls of the room where he lay, all his latest pictures were nailed up, forming a kind of halo for him, so that the radiance of the genius that shone

In his paintings, drawings, and studies, van Gogh depicted the streets, fields, and meadows of Auvers, as well as the 17th-century Château de Léry; the town hall across from the Ravoux Inn; the spiraling, wooden stairway leading up to rue Daubigny; and the Romanesque church (opposite) perched on a hillside near the wheatfields.

from them made his death seem even more grievous to the artists. On the bier there was a plain white sheet and the sunflowers he loved so much. Nearby, too, his easel, his camp stool, and his brushes had been laid on the ground in front of the coffin."

In the small Auvers cemetery, under a bed of ivy strewn with sunflowers, van Gogh lies next to Theo, who survived his brother by a mere six months.

Auvers-sur-Oise

Auvers-sur-Oise is about twenty-two miles northwest of Paris. The picturesque charm of Auvers' narrow winding streets, ivy-draped stone walls, and old shuttered farmhouses has not diminished with the passing of time.

⚜ How To Get There

By Car

From Paris, take autoroute A15 (direction Cergy-Pontoise). Turn off at Exit #7, taking RN 184 toward Amiens-Beauvais. Exit at Méry-sur-Oise and follow the signs for Auvers-sur-Oise.

By Train

Tel: (33) 01 53 90 20 20
Trains depart daily from Paris's Gare du Nord and Gare Saint-Lazare. Change to the local line either at Pontoise, Valmondois, or Saint-Ouen-l'Aumone. The scenic ride through the French countryside takes about seventy minutes, depending on your route and time of departure. Round trip fare is 57 francs. Tickets should be purchased at the windows marked Banlieue (suburbs). Before you board, don't forget to validate (*composter*) your ticket at the orange post-like structures located throughout the train stations (often near the tracks). Failure to do so will result in a fine from train inspectors on board. Trains to the suburbs leave frequently, some just minutes apart. If you are early to the station, do not assume that the train waiting at your designated platform is leaving for your destination. Board as closely as possible to departure time.

⚜ Tourist Office

Manoir des Colombières
Rue de la Sansonne
95430 Auvers-sur-Oise
Tel: (33) 01 30 36 10 06
The office provides free tourist brochures and maps listing walking tours and sites painted by van Gogh, Cézanne, and Daubigny. For sale are postcards, posters, and books about Auvers and its artists. Organized walking tours of the village are available (French language only).
HOURS: Open daily from 9:30 a.m. to 12 p.m. and 2 p.m. to 6 p.m.

⚜ House and Studio of Vincent van Gogh

Ravoux Inn/House of van Gogh (Auberge Ravoux)

Place de la Mairie
95430 Auvers-sur-Oise
Tel: (33) 01 30 36 60 60
Fax: (33) 01 30 36 60 61
Information and Reservations:
http://www.vangogh.integra.fr
E mail: vangogh@integra.fr
The Ravoux Inn is located across from the town hall (*mairie*), a short walk from the train station along rue du Général de Gaulle. The main entrance is across from the Tourist Office at 8, rue de la Sansonne. The modest entry fee includes access to van Gogh's attic room, the Dutch painter Anton Hirschig's room, a slide show, and a passport for the House of van Gogh—a small, informative illustrated book about van Gogh, the inn, and Auvers-sur-Oise. Temporary exhibitions are also held, in keeping with van Gogh's wish to one day exhibit his works in a cafe. A bookshop offers a wide selection of volumes about van Gogh and artists' cafes, posters, postcards, and gift items, including reproductions of the absinthe glass and decanter depicted in van Gogh's painting *Absinthe* (1887).

HOURS: Open every day but Monday from 10 a.m. to 6 p.m.
ENTRY FEE: 30 francs for individuals; 60 francs for families.

Other Services

Available for purchase is a replica of the key to van Gogh's attic room. This key, which comes with a House of van Gogh passport and a book about van Gogh's last stay at Ravoux Inn, entitles the visitor to unlimited free entry to the House of van Gogh. It can also be exchanged for a meal at Ravoux Inn. Proceeds go toward the operation of the House of van Gogh, a private historic monument. The original key to van Gogh's room was sold at Christie's in New York in 1996 for $1,600. Key price for one person: 380 francs; two persons: 680 francs; four persons: 1,290 francs

Dining

Tel: (33) 01 30 36 60 63
At the Ravoux Inn, visitors can enjoy traditional, home-style French meals and country wines in the ambience of a 19th century artists' cafe, complete with its original checkered gray tile floors, antique tables, straw-seated chairs, wine racks, and zinc bar. Custom glassware and tableware includes Villeroy and Boch china decorated with a leaf garland border created by this Luxembourg company in 1890. Coincidentally, van Gogh made his only sale, of *The Red Vineyard*, to a Boch family member. The house specialty is *gigot de sept heures*, a popular dish in which a leg of lamb is cooked for seven hours in a casserole with wine, herbs, and vegetables. Other offerings, served at the table in 19th-century style, include rabbit terrine, duck, salmon, and beef filet.
Fixed price: 145 francs for a two-course meal; 185 francs for a three-course meal. Seating is limited to forty. Ravoux Inn is listed in guides such as Michelin, Gault-Millau, and Best Tables of Europe.

The same menu is served at the adjacent *guinguette*, inspired by van Gogh's painting *The Restaurant Sirene at Asnières* (1887) and reminiscent of the popular 19th-century establishments frequented by artists. Often located by the riverside, *guinguettes* offered food, drink, and lively entertainment. With seating for sixty, this facility is particularly suited for groups.

HOURS: Both eateries are open Tuesday to Sunday, 12 p.m. to 3:30 p.m. and 7:30 p.m. to 11 p.m. Non-stop service on Sunday from 12 p.m. to 5 p.m. Reservations are recommended for lunch and dinner.

☙ House and Studio of Charles-François Daubigny

Villa des Vallées
61, rue Daubigny
95430 Auvers-sur-Oise
Tel: (33) 01 34 48 03 03
Fax: (33) 01 30 36 79 42
Daubigny's house and studio, where he lived from 1862 to 1878, has been restored to its original 19th-century appearance by his great-grandson, Daniel Raskin. It is just steps away from the Ravoux Inn, where van Gogh would spend his final days three decades later.
HOURS: Open from April 10 to November 1 from 2 p.m. to 6:30 p.m. Closed Monday and Tuesday.
ENTRY FEE: 25 francs

Daubigny Museum
Manoir des Colombières
Rue de la Sansonne
95430 Auvers-sur-Oise
Located in the same building as the Tourist Office
Tel: (33) 01 30 36 80 20
On display are 19th-century paintings, watercolors, drawings, and engravings by Charles-François Daubigny, his son Karl, Paul Cézanne, Dr. Paul Gachet (who signed his works with the pseudonym Paul van Ryssel), Jean François

Millet, and lesser known painters. Also contemporary art exhibitions.
HOURS: Open in the winter from 2 p.m. to 5:30 p.m; in the summer from 2:30 p.m. to 6:30 p.m. Closed Monday and Tuesday.

☙ Auvers-sur-Oise Sites

Absinthe Museum (Musée Absinthe)
44, rue Calle
95430 Auvers-sur-Oise
Tel: (33) 01 30 36 83 26
Absinthe, the potent green liqueur favored by 19th-century artists, is the subject of this intimate little museum that tells the story of the "green muse" through old absinthe glasses, bottles, posters, engravings, reproductions of paintings by van Gogh, Edgar Degas, and Edouard Manet depicting absinthe drinkers, a recreation of a 19th-century bar and cafe, and other absinthe-related objects.
HOURS: Open June through September, Wednesday to Sunday from 11 a.m. to 6 p.m. October through May open Saturday and Sunday only.
ENTRY FEE: 25 francs; 6 to 14 years, 10 francs; Under 6 years, free.

Château of Auvers-sur-Oise (Château de Léry)
Rue de Léry
95430 Auvers-sur-Oise
Tel: (33) 01 34 48 48 48
Fax: (33) 01 34 48 48 51
http://www.chateau-auvers.fr
The restored 17th-century Château de Léry, behind which van Gogh reputedly attempted suicide, offers an excellent 90-minute audio-visual presentation of the Impressionist era, incorporating the latest special-effects technology. Visitors walk through the streets of 19th-century Paris, view the works of the Impressionists and the sites they painted, watch the French can-can in a dance hall with Henri de Toulouse-Lautrec, board a train to the coun-

tryside, and brush shoulders with notables such as Degas, Renoir, and Zola, among other illuminating adventures.
HOURS: Open from November through March, from 10 a.m. to 6 p.m; April through October, from 10:30 a.m. to 7:30 p.m. Closed Monday, except June through September.
ENTRY FEE: 60 francs; 6 to 25 years, 40 francs; under 6, free; over 60, 50 francs; family discounts.

The Church at Auvers
The Romanesque-Gothic Notre Dame Church, with an impressive bell tower that is characteristic of the region, is perched on the hillside overlooking Auvers-sur-Oise at the intersection of rue Daubigny and rue Émile Bernard. Given to the nuns of St. Vincent de Senlis by Louis VI in 1131, it is the subject of van Gogh's painting, *The Church at Auvers*. Every May and June the church hosts concerts during the Auvers-sur-Oise International Music Festival.
HOURS: Open daily from 9 a.m. to 6 p.m.

The Cemetery and Wheatfields
Beyond the church at the end of rue Émile Bernard lies the modest cemetery where van Gogh and his brother Theo are buried. Their ivy-covered graves have become a shrine for art lovers from around the world. Also buried here are some lesser-known Auvers painters, including Léonide Bourges, one of Daubigny's pupils. Surrounded by the wheatfields that appear frequently in van Gogh's Auvers paintings, the cemetery is not far from the spot where he painted his *Wheat Field with Crows*.

Dr. Gachet's House

78, rue du Dr. Gachet
95430 Auvers-sur-Oise
Dr. Paul Ferdinand Gachet
(1828–1909), the homeopathic
physician, Impressionist patron and
amateur painter and engraver who
cared for van Gogh during his short
stay at Auvers, purchased this former
girls' boarding school in 1872.
During the last quarter of the nineteenth century, the property was a
gathering place for many of the
most illustrious painters of the time.
Van Gogh, Paul Cézanne, Camille
Pissarro, Claude Monet, and
Auguste Renoir all passed through
these doors. Van Gogh painted in
Gachet's garden and dined here once
or twice a week. Now a private residence, the house looks much the
same today, but for the chickens,
goats, rabbits, and dogs that once
roamed the property. Van Gogh
painted *Portrait of Dr. Gachet* here,
as well as *Dr. Gachet's Garden in
Auvers* and *Marguerite Gachet in the
Garden*, all on display at the Musée
d'Orsay in Paris. He also printed his

one and only engraving, *L'Homme à
la Pipe*, on Gachet's printing press.
Dr. Gachet's extraordinary collection
of paintings now form the Gachet
Donation at the Musée d'Orsay.

Pendu's House

Intersection of rue François
Coppée, rue de la Cherielle, and rue
des Meulières.
Paul Cézanne (1839–1906) lived for
two years at 66, rue Rémy, not far
from Dr. Gachet. Between 1872 and
1874 he made several paintings in
the area, including *Dr. Gachet's
House, Crossroads at the rue Rémy,*
and *Pendu's House*, all on display at
the Musée d'Orsay. It was at Auvers
that Cézanne first painted outdoors,
adopted simple country scenes as
his subject, experimented with
Impressionism, and laid the ground-
work for his future masterpieces.
Probably the best known of
Cézanne's Auvers paintings, *Pendu's
House* took its name from the
Breton man living there at the time.

At the cemetery at Auvers-sur-Oise,
van Gogh is buried next to his
brother Theo.

Scenic Walks

The countryside depicted in van Gogh's, Daubigny's, and Cézanne's paintings unfolds with a leisurely stroll through the village. Color reproductions of their canvases are posted at the many sites where they set up their easels. A convenient starting point is the old wooden staircase opposite the Tourist Office which was the subject of van Gogh's *Stairway at Auvers*. Other notable landmarks include Ossip Zadkine's towering bronze statue of van Gogh, located in the Parc van Gogh along rue du Général de Gaulle, and a 1905 bronze bust of Daubigny by Léon Fagel that stands below the church wall. Across from the train station on rue du Général de Gaulle, a reproduction of one of van Gogh's favorite paintings, *Daubigny's Garden*, marks the site of Daubigny's other residence at Auvers. An iron gate allows only a limited view of the now overgrown garden. Galleries throughout the village show the work of the many painters and sculptors who still live and work here in the tradition of their famous forefathers.

Walking Tours

Organized walking tours of the village are available Sundays at 3 p.m. from April to October. Departure is from the Auvers Tourist Office (see above). French language only.
FEE: 30 francs.

✤Dining

(In addition to the excellent restaurant at Ravoux Inn)

Château of Auvers-sur-Oise
Rue de Léry
95430 Auvers-sur-Oise
Tel: (33) 01 34 48 48 48
Les Canotiers restaurant serves lunch in a lovely 17th-century stone-walled orangerie and an adjacent, less formal *guinguette*. At the

guinguette, dinner is served only for groups, with a 20-person minimum. Menus at 98 and 135 francs offer dishes such as lamb sauteed with eggplant, fish with fresh herbs, and a selection of salads and desserts.
HOURS: Les Canotiers is open every day but Monday from 12 p.m. to 2:30 p.m. An outdoor bistro serves salads and pastries on weekends and holidays from April to November, 12 p.m. to 2:30 p.m.
Reservations: (33) 01 34 48 05 05
Groups: (33) 01 34 48 48 50

Hostellerie du Nord
6, rue du Général de Gaulle
95430 Auvers-sur-Oise
Tel: (33) 01 30 36 70 74
Fax: (33) 01 30 36 72 75
Built in the 17th century, this amiable restaurant was formerly a rest stop on the horse-and-carriage route north from Paris. Daubigny and Cézanne were among its many patrons. The painter and engraver Léonide Bourges, who studied with Daubigny and Corot, lived here during her stay in Auvers. The Hostellerie has a garden terrace with a lovely view of the church. Menus at 120 and 190 francs include salmon, filet of beef, duck with strawberries, foie gras, cheeses, salads, and desserts.
HOURS: Closed Sunday night and Monday.

Au Verre Placide
20, rue du Général de Gaulle
95430 Auvers-sur-Oise
Tel: (33) 01 34 48 02 11
Formerly known as Cafe Partois, this restaurant/brasserie was a favorite haunt of Daubigny, Cézanne, and Pissarro. Located across from the train station, it also organizes contemporary painting exhibitions. Menus at 105 and 135 francs include filet of roast duck, pork confit with ginger and rice, salads, cheeses, and desserts.
HOURS: Open every day for lunch and dinner.

✤ Accommodations

Auvers-sur-Oise is close enough to Paris to allow for a convenient day trip. Check the board outside the Auvers station for return times to Pontoise. Change at Pontoise to Paris's Gare Du Nord or Gare St-Lazare. There are currently no hotels in Auvers-sur-Oise (population 6,500), but there are several pleasant bed-and-breakfast options in local homes:

La Ramure
M. and Mme. Amaniera
38, rue du Montcel
95430 Auvers-sur-Oise
Tel: (33) 01 30 36 79 32
A 19th-century building and garden located near the church, this cozy bed-and-breakfast has three rooms, each with a private bath and furnished with country antiques. Prices are 250, 350, and 400 francs. Breakfast included.

M. and Mme. Caffin
4, rue Marceau
95430 Auvers-sur-Oise
Tel: (33) 01 30 36 70 26
This rustic farmhouse has three rooms with showers. Prices are 260 francs per night for two persons; 210 francs per night for one person. Breakfast included.

M. and Mme. Baba
3 *bis*, rue du Clos Sermon
95430 Auvers-sur-Oise
Tel: (33) 01 30 36 16 63
Not far from the House of van Gogh, a modern apartment with a bath and kitchen is available for 280 francs per night for two persons; 200 francs per night for one person. Breakfast is included. View of the Oise River.

♣ Nearby Accommodations

Novotel Château de Maffliers
Allée des Marroniers
9560 Maffliers
Tel: (33) 01 34 08 35 35
Fax: (33) 01 34 69 97 49
This peaceful, three-star hotel in
Maffliers, about a ten-minute drive
from Auvers, occupies a lovely old
manor house. Rates are 620 francs
per night for two persons; 570
francs per night for one person.

♣ Short Excursions

Pontoise

This scenic town, where the painter
Camille Pissarro (1830–1903) lived
from 1872 to 1884, is just a thirteen
minute train ride from Auvers-sur-
Oise. A leading figure of the
Impressionist school and mentor to
artists like van Gogh, Cézanne,
Degas, Gauguin, and Seurat,
Pissarro is noted for his intimate
rural landscapes depicting peasants
in harmony with nature. While
Daubigny preferred riverscapes,
Pissarro wandered the Oise Valley
with his easel, often stopping to
paint in the Valhermeil quarter of
Auvers. Throughout Pontoise are
the sites and landmarks, orchards,
fields, and gardens that inspired his
works and those of Cézanne and
others. "Pissarro has probably left
his Impressionism on all of us,"
Cézanne said.

Musée Pissarro and Musée
Tavet display works by the
Impressionists and contemporaries
of Pissarro such as Honoré Daumier
and Gustave Caillebotte, who lived
in the region. Information available
at the Pontoise Tourist Office.

Pontoise Tourist Office
Place du Petit Martroy
Tel: (33) 01 30 38 24 45

Valmondois

The first train stop after Auvers-sur-
Oise, this picturesque little village
awakened Daubigny's lifelong love
of nature. He spent his early childhood here with a foster mother and
often returned to paint the beautiful
countryside around the banks of the
Oise River. Valmondois was also
home to the painter and caricaturist
Honoré Daumier and the Fauve
painter Maurice de Vlaminck, who
painted along the route from
Auvers-sur-Oise to L'Isle-Adam during the early 20th century. Cézanne
also set up his easel in Valmondois.

Oise Valley (Val d'Oise) Tourist Office
Tel: (33) 01 30 29 51 00 OR
    (33) 01 34 69 67 05

**Museums in Paris with works by
van Gogh and Daubigny:**

- ♣ **Musée d'Orsay**
  Van Gogh, Daubigny
- ♣ **Musée Rodin**
  Van Gogh
- ♣ **Bibliothèque Nationale**
  engravings by Daubigny

Jean-François Millet: *The Gleaners*
(1857), Musée d'Orsay, Paris;
photo © Erich Lessing, Art
Resource, New York.

Jean-François Millet

Best known for his depictions of peasant life in Barbizon, a picturesque village south of Paris that became a refuge for such landscape painters as Corot, Rousseau, and Daubigny, Jean-François Millet inspired near-religious devotion in many painters who followed. His commitment to seeking truth in painting, coupled with his reverence for nature and man's inescapable connection to it, earned him the admiration of van Gogh, Pissarro, Cézanne, and others. Born in 1814 to a prosperous peasant family in the Norman hamlet of Gruchy, Millet spent his youth reading, sketching, and working on his father's farm. Having moved to Paris in 1837 on a municipal art scholarship, he copied old masters in the Louvre and developed a passion for the works of Poussin and Michelangelo, with whom he shared an instinctive classicism. Never feeling at home in the cosmopolitan city, the solitary peasant returned to Normandy to establish himself as a portrait painter, but was back in Paris by 1841. He began living with Catherine Lemaire, a Norman servant who later became his wife. While Millet participated frequently in the Salons, reaction to his work was often mixed. The peasant was a controversial subject in the wake of the Revolution of 1848; consequently, Millet's proletariat subject matter met with harsh criticism from conservatives who cast him as a socialist revolutionary. He nevertheless stayed true to his view of himself as an artist who rose above politics and Salon aesthetics to create a universal art sympathetic to the human condition. In 1849, fleeing both the political turmoil in Paris and a cholera epidemic that claimed tens of thousands of lives, Millet and his family set down roots in the small village of Barbizon near the Fontainebleau forest. He remained for nearly three decades until his death in 1875, and it was there that he produced his most celebrated paintings, drawings, and pastels.

Jean-François Millet: *Self-portrait*, Musée du Louvre, Paris; Giraudon/Art Resource, New York.

Millet in Barbizon
1849–1875
The Peasant Painter

"Take off your shoes, for the place where you are standing
is Holy Ground," wrote Vincent van Gogh after viewing a
collection of pastels by Jean-François Millet.

Millet undoubtedly found his own holy ground in 1849,
when he first set foot in the small village of Barbizon, situated between the magnificent Fontainebleau forest and the
broad Bière plain, about twenty-five miles south of Paris.
"I see in it more than charm," he wrote of the countryside.
"I clearly perceive the haloes of the dandelions, the sun shed-
ding over the earth beneath, far away into the distance, its
heavenly glory. But there on the plain, I also see the steaming
horses at the plow, and on stony land I see an exhausted
man, whose grunts have been audible since morning, stretch-
ing for a moment and trying to catch his breath. The drama
is wrapped in splendors."

Millet's biographer, Alfred Sensier, wrote of Millet's and
an artist friend's instant enchantment with the forest and the
village–inhabited mainly by farm workers, woodcutters, and
quarrymen: "They had reached such a pitch of over-excite-
ment that they were quite unable to work: the proud majesty
of the old trees, the virgin state of rocks and heather, . . .
and verdant landscapes, all these intoxicated them with their
beauty and their smell. . . . There Millet found his country
people at work; he saw his epic dreams taking shape before
his eyes . . . he felt the spirit of his forefathers stir within
him. He became a peasant again."

The artist initially rented a barn for use as a studio and
lodged at the Ganne Inn, the legendary gathering place for
the hundreds of landscape painters who flocked to the
bohemian art colony in the mid-nineteenth century in search
of a simple life in communion with nature. Now restored as
a museum, the inn hosted one of the greatest concentrations

Millet himself often wore wooden
peasant shoes (opposite) called
sabots that kept his feet dry while he
walked the weatherbeaten earth.

The gray exterior of Millet's Barbizon cottage is brightened by an abundant courtyard garden and an overgrowth of red ivy and clematis. The painter's love of nature was so intense that the pruning of the foliage was said to have caused him actual pain.

of creative talent in a single time and place; the masters Camille Corot and Théodore Rousseau were among its more illustrious guests. A bucolic tableau of gnarled linden trees and wisteria-draped stone walls, red-tile-roofed cottages and courtyard gardens, Barbizon appears much the same now as in 1824, when the painters Claude Aligny and Philippe Le Dieu first stumbled upon it and spread the news of its beauty to their artist friends in Paris.

Open air painting was enjoying a vogue, aided by the packaging of paint in tubes, an innovation of the 1830s that facilitated working outdoors. The opening of the railroad to Fontainebleau in 1849 also contributed to the revival of French landscape painting in the nineteenth century.

By the time Millet moved to Barbizon, he had decided to devote himself to scenes from nature and rural life reminiscent of his childhood. The robust, black-bearded artist set up housekeeping with his family, who had arrived by stagecoach from Paris, in a small peasant cottage that still sits unpretentiously along the main street. Inside, a humble studio, the first of three rooms, greets the visitor with worn wooden floors, carved furniture, Millet's large oak easels and plaster casts, and numerous engravings of his works. A barn across the garden, which has been replaced by a local restaurant, served as a studio and additional living space for Millet, his wife, and their nine children.

Millet rose early to tend his garden, dressed in an old straw hat and sailor's blouse. Then he wandered off to observe peasants at work in the fields before returning in the afternoons to his studio to distill his impressions on canvas. Unlike his Barbizon contemporaries, Millet rarely painted directly from nature, but instead made quick sketches that he later developed in the studio. When terrible migraines disrupted his work, he retired to the forest for respite.

In Barbizon, he produced many of his celebrated paintings, including *The Sower*, *The Gleaners*, and *The Angelus*, a solemn image of a peasant couple bowed in prayer that became popular through reproductions on dinnerware, music boxes, and other quotidian objects.

The wooden shoes piled in a corner of the studio are a reminder of Millet's affection for simple men and women who, despite their toilsome labors, existed in harmony with nature, free of the mechanization and superficiality of urban life. His wedding chest, a glass cabinet with ceramic cider pitchers from Brittany, and numerous landscapes by fellow Barbizon artists are also displayed here.

Deeply connected to his own peasant origins, Millet differed from other Barbizon painters in his belief that the beauty of a landscape was inseparable from the people who lived in it. Millet, often called the Rustic Michelangelo, endowed his rural subjects with a solemn austerity and an epic grandeur formerly reserved for history paintings. In all his works, in which the peasant's devotion to his earthly labors takes on religious significance, there is evidence of Millet's moralizing vision, his reverence for the human struggle.

"It is the human side that touches me most in art," he declared, " . . . you see coming forth from a little path a wretched form laden with faggots . . . you see figures digging with spade or mattock . . . one of them from time to time wiping his brow with the back of his hand. It is

The worn, Renaissance-style arm-chair near the window of the dining room is where Millet often sat, looking onto his garden and reading the Bible or Virgil for inspiration. The hand-painted grandfather clock remains perpetually set to 6 a.m., the hour of Millet's death.

there that I find the true humanity, the grand poetry."

Millet's presence lingers among the dining room's eclectic antique furniture; his paint-caked palette and birth and death certificates; a small, faded leather bible; and several photographs of the artist himself, possessed of a palpable dignity and intensity.

A rush-seated chair from Normandy and an oak cabinet carved by Millet's brother flank the plaster fireplace, orna-mented with medallion portraits of Benjamin Franklin, Robespierre, and others. On the walls are etchings and sketches by Théodore Rousseau, Jules Dupré, Charles

Jacque, and other Barbizon artists, as well as a ceramic plate bearing a reproduction of *The Angelus*.

Adjoining the dining area is a spacious room dominated by a large fireplace that served as Millet's kitchen.

The writer Jules Claretie described the intimacy of the Millet family's life at Barbizon: "On the right side of the street, in going toward the forest, one can see around a table, lighted by a lamp, a family patriarchally grouped. The mother and the father are there, the children are working, the girls sewing… Sometimes the father, who is reading to himself, finishes his reading aloud. They listen without raising their heads. The father is a large. . . . man, young still, with gentle expression, calm and severe at the same time . . . something of the peasant and of the Quaker. He is silent and usually dreaming."

Millet's domestic happiness was overshadowed by his long struggle for recognition and his continual financial worries. After finishing *The Angelus* in 1859, he confided to Sensier: "We have only wood for two or three days more . . . I am suffering and sad."

In the dining room hang works by Millet's fellow Barbizon artists, including one by his close friend, Rousseau.

Jean-François Millet: *The Angelus*
(1859), Musée d'Orsay, Paris; photo
© Erich Lessing, Art Resource,
New York.

Millet's art reflects his melancholy temperament, rooted
in his devout upbringing and a fatalism that embraced the
harsh realities of peasant life, the inevitable passage of time,
and man's insignificance before nature. Conservative critics
saw Millet's toiling, unidealized peasants as images of political
protest, but the artist held little hope for social reform. In an
attempt to dispel hostile criticism of his work, he proclaimed:
"They believe that they will make me bend, that they will
impose upon me the art of the Salons. Ah, no! Peasant I was
born, peasant I shall die. I wish to say that which I feel. I
have things to describe as I have seen them, and I will remain
upon my soil without retreating a *sabot's* length."

Landscapes dominated Millet's final years, which were
marked by an extraordinary productivity despite the growing
severity of his headaches. After 1865, Millet worked increas-

ingly in pastels, whose integration of line and pure color foreshadow the work of Edgar Degas. But it is perhaps his meticulous drawings, whose expressive light and dark contrasts inspired Georges Seurat, which have become his greatest legacy.

It was not until the last decade of his life that his reputation became established through increased exhibitions and sales of his work. He especially found favor with American collectors introduced to him by the Boston painter William Morris Hunt, his friend and Barbizon neighbor.

Here, in his Barbizon home, Millet died of a brain tumor in 1875 at the age of sixty-one. "Too soon," he said, his family gathered around him. "Just as I am beginning to see clearly into nature and art." Upon his death, a newspaper article stated that "he was searching for the essence, and he found it." He lies next to Rousseau in a cemetery on the edge of the forest, under a stark white stone, in the earth he loved so well.

Barbizon

Barbizon is about twenty-five miles southeast of Paris, in the department of Seine-et-Marne in the Île de France region. The village is lined with cobblestone sidewalks, 19th-century stone farmhouses and ivy- and wisteria-draped stone walls. While its old stables have disappeared and it is now home to eighteen galleries, eighteen hotels and restaurants, and a number of contemporary artists, Barbizon has maintained an idyllic rural charm. The legendary art colony there attracted artists from all over Europe, as well as the Americans William Morris Hunt (one of Millet's disciples and a collector of his work) and George Inness, a noted 19th-century American landscape painter.

☙ How to Get There

By Car

From Paris, the trip to Barbizon takes about an hour. Take autoroute A6 in the direction of Lyon. Exit at Fontainebleau, then at Barbizon.

By Train

Tel: (33) 08 36 35 35 39
Trains depart hourly from Paris's Gare de Lyon station to Melun, the closest city to Barbizon (which does not have its own station). The train will be travelling in the direction of La Roche Migennes. The ride through the French countryside is about twenty-five to forty-eight minutes; round trip fare is 86 francs. Tickets should be purchased at the windows marked Banlieu (suburbs). Don't forget to validate (composter) your ticket at the orange post-like structures located throughout the train stations (often near the tracks). Failure to do so will result in a fine from train inspectors on board.

Taxis

Taxis Melun
(to and from Barbizon)
Tel: (33) 01 64 52 51 50
Taxis Fontainebleau-Avon
(to and from Barbizon)
Tel: (33) 01 64 22 78 05
Taxis are usually waiting at the Melun station. The fifteen-mininute ride is about 90 francs one way. The twenty-minute taxi ride from Fontainebleau-Avon station (two stops after Melun) to Barbizon is about 100 francs one way. Taxi prices vary according to the particular day and time; fares are often more expensive on weekends.

☙ Tourist Offices

Barbizon Tourist Office

55, Grande Rue
77630 Barbizon
Tel: (33) 01 60 66 41 87
Fax: (33) 01 60 66 42 46
http/www.barbizon-france
The tourist office, located in the painter Théodore Rousseau's former home, offers free brochures and maps of Barbizon, Fontainebleau forest, and the surrounding area. Also available is a special "picnic in painter's country" package for 180 francs per person which includes a free visit to the Ganne Inn, a picnic in the forest, and a beginners' painting class with a painter from Barbizon (materials provided).
HOURS: Wednesday through Friday from 1 p.m. to 5 p.m.; Saturday and Sunday from 11 a.m. to 12:30 p.m. and 2 p.m. to 5 p.m.

Regional Tourist Office (Maison Departementale du Tourisme de Seine-et-Marne)

11, rue Royale
77300 Fontainebleau
Tel: (33) 01 60 39 60 39
Fax: (33) 01 60 39 60 40
This tourist office in nearby Fontainebleau oversees the department of Seine-et-Marne, which includes Barbizon. It is another good source for information about Barbizon, as well as other attractions in the area.

☙House and Studio of Jean-François Millet

House and Studio of Jean-François Millet

27, Grand Rue
77630 Barbizon
Tel: (33) 01 60 66 21 55
Millet's home and studio are situated along the picturesque main street in Barbizon. The amiable Mr. Richard, who oversees Millet's home and studio, is full of information on Millet and Barbizon's artistic heritage.
HOURS: The museum is open every day but Tuesday, from 10 a.m. to 12:30 p.m. and from 2 p.m. to 6 p.m. (5 p.m. in the winter).
ENTRY FEE: Admission is free.

☙ Barbizon Sites

Ganne Inn
The Municipal Museum of the Barbizon School

92, Grande Rue
77630 Barbizon
Tel: (33) 01 60 66 22 27
Fax: (33) 01 60 66 22 96
The famous gathering place of the Barbizon artists opened its doors in 1824, when a local tailor and grocer, François Ganne, and his wife, Edmée, expanded their quarters into a barn-like inn providing food and lodging to hundreds of painters who flocked here during the mid-nineteenth century. The Gannes' rudimentary lodgings, which provided the setting for the Goncourt brothers' novel Manette Salomon, were described in an art magazine of the period as comprising a "single storey above the ground floor, a perfectly plain façade with a carriage gate, through which you can see right into a courtyard dotted with puddles and

dung-hills, on top of which old gallic cockerels sing their hearts out . . . ." Here, within the cozy confines of pale blue walls and low, white-beamed ceilings, the Barbizon painters found camaraderie and sanctuary. More than 100 drawings and paintings uncovered several years ago on the walls and furniture of the inn weave a pictorial tale of the artists' lives in Barbizon. Each morning the inn's artists set out to paint directly from nature, depicting the landscape in varying light and seasons. One anonymous wall painting portrays a painter leaving to work in the forest, carrying on his back a folding stool, a parasol, and sacks containing a picnic lunch, a paint box, and two canvases for both morning and evening effect. On rainy days, the artists honed their skills on the inn's bare walls, pine panels, and furniture. Throughout the ground floor of Ganne Inn, reconstituted with its original rustic furniture, are examples of the Barbizon painters' genius. A wooden partition dividing

the artists dining room, for instance, is adorned with landscapes and fanciful floral and bird ornamentation by Rousseau, Narcisse Diaz de la Pena, and lesser-known artists. In the officers room, where soldiers from the military camp at Fontainebleau dined, an enormous wardrobe displays village scenes and forest landscapes, while garlands of roses by Diaz frame a mirror above the fireplace. One can imagine the painters gathered around a large oak table, having returned from the forest to critique each other's work. After dinner, they joked, discussed art, and invited newcomers to smoke the "peace pipe," judging from the color of the smoke curls whether the novice was a classicist or a colorist. Sometimes the masters—fun-loving, fatherly Corot, the intense, black-bearded Millet, and Diaz, whose wooden leg announced his arrival—condescended to take coffee with amateur artists, who regarded them with god-like veneration. The story of Barbizon and Ganne Inn is also one of great faith

Jean-François Millet's home and studio are situated along the main street in Barbizon.

and friendship. In their struggle for acceptance, the Barbizon artists frequently offered each other moral and financial support. One of the first to arrive at Ganne Inn in 1830, Corot was especially generous to his penniless pupils and colleagues. Noted for his lyrical paintings of the landscape at twilight, he was profoundly inspired by the Fontainebleau forest. Rousseau, like Millet and many other painters, also stayed briefly at Ganne Inn before buying his own home in the village. Upstairs, where the painters shared several bedrooms, specialists from the restoration departments of France's museums have discovered images of animals, villagers, local landscapes, and the painters themselves on the walls beneath layers of whitewash. (Most of these cannot be attributed to specific artists.) The upstairs rooms now serve as exhibition space for works from the Municipal Museum of the Barbizon School. The collection of more than 300 works includes landscapes of the forest and village by Corot and Rousseau, as well as works by Millet. HOURS: The museum is open every day but Tuesday from 10 a.m. to 12:30 p.m. and 2 p.m. to 6 p.m. (5 p.m. October 1 through March 30) ENTRY FEE: 35 francs

Théodore Rousseau House and Studio

55, Grand Rue
77630 Barbizon
Tel: (33) 01 60 66 22 38
Théodore Rousseau's home is located along the main street in Barbizon. He lived here for about 20 years until his death in 1867. The space is now occupied by the Barbizon tourist office. Rousseau also rented an adjacent barn for use as a studio, which was converted into a chapel at the end of the century. Rousseau's true domain, however, was the forest. Recognized by many as the leader of the Barbizon school and the most significant

landscape artist of his generation, Rousseau depicted nature with extraordinary accuracy, rendering trees, boulders, leaves, moss, and bark in minute detail. Influenced by the 19th-century crosscurrents of Romanticism and scientific observation, he created art dictated by his belief that man and nature were one. Such paintings as *The Forest in Winter at Sunset* (now in The Metropolitan Museum of Art, New York), which Rousseau considered his masterpiece, reveal his understanding of the qualities of light and the passage of time, as well as his Romantic tendency to emotionalize nature. Although he was known as *le grand réfusé*, the great rejected artist, after suffering numerous rejections from the Salons (which did not recognize landscape painting as a traditional art form), Rousseau nevertheless inspired a generation of younger landscape artists, who often accompanied him on instructive walks through the forest.
HOURS: Open Wednesday through Friday from 1 p.m. to 5 p.m.; Saturday and Sunday from 11 a.m. to 12:30 p.m. and 2 p.m. to 5 p.m.

Other Artists' Homes

Along the main street in Barbizon are the former homes of painters Charles Jacque (1813–1894) and Narcisse-Virgile Diaz de la Peña (1807–1876), and sculptor Antoine Louis Barye (1796–1875), each marked by a plaque on the stone wall facing the street. Millet's friend, Jacque, painted mainly in Barbizon and became known for his paintings of farmyards and sheep. Diaz, an artist of Spanish origin noted for his romantic figure paintings, was one of Rousseau's most ardent disciples. He is best remembered for his richly painted landscapes of the Fontainebleau forest, created during the 1850s. A close friend of Rousseau, Barye was an animal sculptor who spent summers

in Barbizon before renting a house here. He made studies of wild animals in Paris's Jardin des Plantes with his friend, Eugène Delacroix.

❧ Special Services

Madame Pascale Nys

Tel: (33) 01 64 49 37 78
Madame Nys, an English- and Spanish-speaking guide, offers tours of Barbizon for groups of up to 20 people. The enthusiastic Madame Nys studied at L'École du Louvre, and is very knowledgeable about French art.
FEE: Full-day tours, 1,000 francs; Half-day tours, 500 francs.

❧ Dining

Hôtellerie du Bas-Bréau

22, Grande Rue
77630 Barbizon
Tel: (33) 01 60 66 40 05
Fax: (33) 01 60 69 22 89
E-mail: basbreau@relaischateaux.fr
Excellent gourmet meals are served in the elegant old-world dining room and garden courtyard of this historic inn. The four-star Relais & Chateaux property hosted many Barbizon artists in the 1830s, when it was known as Monsieur Siron's inn. Specialties include foie gras, lobster fricassée, roast lamb, veal, and fish dishes prepared with herbs from the hotel's garden. À la carte items are priced up to 360 francs; menu at 400 francs.
HOURS: Lunch from 12 p.m. to 2:30 p.m.; dinner from 8 p.m. to 9:30 p.m.

Hostellerie les Pléiades

21, Grand Rue
77630 Barbizon
Tel: (33) 01 60 66 40 25
Fax: (33) 01 60 66 41 68
One of the finest restaurants in Barbizon occupies the former home of the landscape painter Charles-François Daubigny, who often stayed at Ganne Inn. Daubigny

painted in the Fontainebleau forest, and was influenced by the Barbizon painters. (See separate chapter on Daubigny's home and studio in Auvers-sur-Oise.) The large dining room has a warm family atmosphere and opens onto an outdoor terrace. The menus at 185 francs and 280 francs include filet of beef, lamb, lobster, gazpacho, foie gras, and mushroom galette.

HOURS: Lunch is served from 12:30 p.m to 2:30 p.m.; dinner from 7:30 p.m. to 10:30 p.m.

Hostellerie la Clé d'Or

73, Grande Rue
77630 Barbizon
Tel: (33) 01 60 66 40 96
Fax: (33) 01 60 66 42 71
This cozy three-star inn has a lovely dining room with a fireplace and a shady garden terrace. À la carte dishes and menus from 170 francs to 230 francs include pigeon, grilled pork, filet of lamb, salmon, sole, and foie gras.

HOURS: Lunch is served from 12 p.m. to 2:30 p.m.; dinner from 7:30 p.m. to 9:30 p.m.

Restaurant l'Angelus

31, Grande Rue
77630 Barbizon
Tel: (33) 01 60 66 40 30
Fax: (33) 01 60 66 42 12
Adjacent to Millet's home and studio, this charming restaurant serves home-cooked meals in a country ambience. There is also a garden terrace. Dishes priced from 60 francs to 131 francs include grilled salmon, duck, filet of beef, salads, and cheeses. Menus range from 175 francs to 230 francs.

HOURS: Lunch from 12:15 p.m. to 2:30 p.m.; dinner from 7:15 p.m. to 9:30 p.m. Closed Tuesday.

La Bohème

35, Grand Rue
77630 Barbizon
Tel: (33) 01 60 66 48 65
This cozy restaurant with a private garden terrace is owned by local painter François Federle. Many of his landscapes adorn the rustic, wood-beamed dining room. Duck and homemade foie gras are the house specialties. Other dishes include onion soup, lamb curry,

Ganne Inn, on the main street in Barbizon, not far from Millet's home and studio, was a famous gathering place for landscape artists during the mid-nineteenth century.

beef bourguignon, and a selection of salads and desserts. The menu is 150 francs; à la carte items range from 45 francs to 125 francs. HOURS: Open for lunch from 12 p.m. to 2 p.m; dinner from 7 p.m. to 11 p.m. (approximately). Closed Sunday night and Monday.

♣ Accommodations

Hôtellerie du Bas-Bréau

22, Grande Rue
77630 Barbizon
Tel: (33) 01 60 66 40 05
Fax: (33) 01 60 69 22 89
E-mail: basbreau@relaischateaux.fr
This four-star, Relais & Chateau property is one of the luxurious old inns of France. Housed in an ivy-covered brown-and-white timbered building near the Fontainebleau forest, Bas Bréau has twenty-one spacious rooms decorated with provincial antiques. Some rooms open onto semi-private terraces with flowerboxes. The cozy sitting room has a timbered ceiling, brick fireplace, and bar. There are lovely courtyards, gardens, tennis courts, and a swimming pool. In the 1830s, when it was owned by one Monsieur Siron, the inn hosted many Barbizon artists, as well as the noted author Robert Louis Stevenson, who wrote his *Forest Notes* here. Siron renamed the inn the Hôtel de l'Exposition in 1867 after mounting an exhibition of Barbizon paintings. Napoleon III and Empress Eugènie stopped to buy a few paintings one day after an excursion in the forest. Room rates range from 900 francs to 2800 francs (suite) and 6000 francs for the Villa Stevenson. Continental breakfast is 100 francs.

Hostellerie les Pléiades

21, Grand Rue
77630 Barbizon
Tel: (33) 01 60 66 40 25
Fax: (33) 01 60 66 41 68
This lovely three-star inn, surrounded by shaded terraces, was the former home of the 19th-century landscape painter Charles-François Daubigny. The white stucco and red tile-roof structure houses 23 comfortable rooms with private baths ranging in price from 210 francs to 550 francs.

Hostellerie la Clé d'Or

73, Grande Rue
77630 Barbizon
Tel: (33) 01 60 66 40 96
Fax: (33) 01 60 66 42 71
This hospitable three-star, stone and shuttered inn across the street from Ganne Inn was a relais de post, or mail coach stop, in the 19th century. It has seventeen rooms, many of which open onto a garden courtyard. They are outfitted with rustic and modern furnishings and either a shower or bath. Prices range from 320 francs to 450 francs for a double room; 230 francs to 310 francs for a single room.

Les Charmettes

40, Grand Rue
77630 Barbizon
Tel: (33) 01 60 66 40 21
Fax: (33) 01 60 66 49 74
This charming timbered hotel was built in 1841 to resemble a Swiss chalet. Formerly the home of Swiss artist Karl Bodmer, the two-star property has twelve comfortable rooms with either a shower or bath. Rates range from 295 francs to 400 francs off season. Prices are slightly higher during June and July. Continental breakfast is 45 francs. Room and board rates are available for three-day minimum stays.

The large, rustic dining room serves traditional French cuisine with menus from 135 francs to 165 francs.

Other Options

There are a number of chambres d'hôtes in the area. They are family-owned guest houses which are the equivalent of American bed-and-breakfasts. Gîtes Ruraux are furnished houses in the countryside which can be rented on a weekly basis at reasonable prices. They are ideal for groups and families. Contact the regional Seine-et-Marne tourist office in Fontainebleau for details (listed on p. 75).

♣ Short Excursions

Fontainebleau Forest

No trip to Barbizon would be complete without a stroll through the magnificent Fontainebleau forest (the second largest in France, covering 62,000 acres), the traditional hunting ground of the kings of France, who retreated from Paris to the nearby Fontainebleau Château. The forest is easily accessible by foot or car from the main street in Barbizon. Trail maps are available at the Fontainebleau and Barbizon tourist offices. Amid giant oaks, pines, and birches, sandstone boulders, shaded glens, picturesque ponds, and paths blanketed with pine needles are such sites as the Gorges of Apremont, the fairies' pond, and the Bas Bréau (a cluster of ancient oaks) which were immortalized by the Barbizon painters. The Gorges of Franchard offer panoramic views. Writers such as George Sand (*Her and Him*), Gustave Flaubert (*Sentimental Education*), and Robert Louis Stevenson (*The Treasure of Franchard*) also responded to the rustic charm of the forest and village and recorded their impressions in their novels and stories. At the edge of the forest along the cow path, at the end of the main street in Barbizon, lies a large boulder embedded with a bronze medallion sculpture of Millet and Rousseau.

Inspired by the Barbizon artists' enthusiasm for nature, the Impressionists Monet, Sisley, Renoir, and Pissarro arrived in Barbizon in the 1860s and painted numerous scenes of the Fontainebleau forest, many of which had been depicted by their Barbizon predecessors. Daubigny, Courbet, Cezanne, and Seurat also painted here.

Chailly-en-Bière

This small village is separated from Barbizon by the vast plain depicted in Millet's *The Angelus* and other works.

Many of the Barbizon artists, including Rousseau and Corot, first came to Chailly to paint, and then moved to Barbizon because it was closer to the Fontainebleau forest. Monet, Renoir, Sisley, and other Impressionists stayed at the Auberge de Cheval Blanc in Chailly in the early 1860s, at the dawn of Impressionism. The Auberge is now a cafe and bar which still bears traces of its historic past; in the back room there are sketches and paintings on the walls depicting forest landscapes, animals, figures, and painters' accessories. This is a de rigueur pilgrimage for dedicated art aficionados.

Millet is buried next to Rousseau at the cemetery in Chailly. His grave is marked by a white cross-mounted stone. Rousseau's grave is marked by a mound of rocks resembling those found in the Fontainebleau forest.

How To Get There
It is best to rent a car to explore Chailly (about six miles from the Melun train station) and other villages around Barbizon.

Fontainebleau

Château de Fontainebleau
The pièce de resistance of this small town, about six miles from Barbizon, is the magnificent Fontainebleau château, dubbed the "house of centuries" by Napoleon. It was the country home to French kings for 700 years from the enthronement of Louis VII in 1137 to the fall of the Second Empire in 1870. In 1530, Francois I converted the medieval castle and hunting lodge into a royal palace. He hired the Italian masters Rosso Fiorentino and Primaticcio, who, along with an international team of painters, sculptors, and artisans, adorned the château with sumptuous stucco and fresco decoration in an Italian Renaissance style known as the "School of Fontainebleau." The interiors, furniture, and the many important paintings, tapestries, and objects on display in the château are a chronicle of the embellishments undertaken by successive kings. Of special interest is the recently restored private apartment of Napoleon I. Six rooms, including the abdication salon, where the emperor relinquished his reign in 1814, are ornamented with gilt panelling, brocade and silk walls, and elaborate Empire furniture.
HOURS: Open daily except Tuesdays, January 1, May 1, and December 25. November through April: 9:30 a.m. to 12:30 p.m. and 2 p.m to 5 p.m. May through October: 9:30 a.m. to 5 p.m. (6 p.m. during July and August).
ENTRY FEE: 35 francs; 23 francs Sundays; free for those 18 years and under.

How To Get There
To drive to Fontainebleau from Paris, take autoroute A6 toward Lyon, and get off at the Fontainebleau exit. Then take the N7 to Fontainebleau.

Trains from Paris's Gare de Lyon station (Banlieu line) stop at Fontainebleau-Avon (about a 40 minute ride; 94 francs round trip). It's a short ride by taxi (about 40 francs one way) or bus (CGEA bus company, direction Fontainebleau Château) to the château.

To explore the nearby Fontainebleau forest, bikes can be rented at the Fontainebleau-Avon station for 80 francs per half day; 120 francs per day, or at the Fontainebleau Tourist Office for 80 francs per half day; 100 francs per day.

Fontainebleau is the best place in the area to rent a car to explore Barbizon, the Fontainebleau forest, and surroundings. These are several car rental agencies in Fontainebleau:

ADA
207, rue Grande,
Tel: (33) 01 60 71 08 81

Avis
185, rue Grande,
Tel: (33) 01 64 22 49 65

Europcar
185, rue Grande,
Tel: (33) 01 64 22 42 62

Hertz
232, rue Grande
Tel: (33) 01 64 22 55 77

Fontainebleau Tourist Office
4, rue Royale
77300 Fontainebleau
Tel: (33) 01 60 74 99 99

Regional Tourist Office (Maison Departementale du Tourisme de Seine-et-Marne)
11, rue Royale
77300 Fontainebleau
Tel: (33) 01 60 39 60 39
Fax: (33) 01 60 39 60 40

Château de Vaux-le-Vicomte

Tel: (33) 01 64 14 41 90
The elegant, Neoclassical Baroque-style Vaux-le-Vicomte château is located about twelve miles northeast of Fontainebleau. In the mid-17th century, Nicolas Fouquet, Louis XIV's Minister of Finance, commissioned the architect Le Vau, the artist Le Brun, and the landscaper Le Notre to build a château for him. Louis XIV was so impressed that he hired the same artists to create Versailles, which bears striking similarities to the much smaller Vaux, one of the most beautiful private châteaux in France.
HOURS: Vaux-le-Vicomte is open from March 11 to November 11 from 10 a.m. to 6 p.m; The château and park are lit up by thousands of candles every Thursday and Saturday evening from 8 p.m. to 12 a.m. from mid-May to mid-October.
ENTRY FEE: 62 francs; 80 francs for visit with candles.

How To Get There

To get to Vaux-le-Vicomte, take the train from Paris's Gare de Lyon station (Banlieu line) to Melun (25 minutes; 86 francs round trip). Taxi fare from the Melun station to the château is about 80 francs one way (100 francs on weekends).

Moret-sur-Loing

The charming medieval fortress town of Moret-sur-Loing, situated between the Fontainebleau forest and the Loing river about twelve miles from Barbizon, has long attracted painters, notably the Impressionist Alfred Sisley, who lived here for ten years until his death in 1899. His home and studio still stand at the corner of Rue Montmartre and rue du Donjon, not far from the Moret church. The narrow, picturesque streets, ancient timbered houses, the canal, and banks of the Loing have changed little since Sisley immortalized them in his paintings.

How To Get There

To get to Moret-sur-Loing by train, leave from Paris's Gare de Lyon station (Banlieu line) to Moret/Veneux-les-Sablons (one stop after Thomery, three stops after Fontainebleau-Avon; about a fifty-minute ride) and walk to the tourist office in the center of town.

Moret Tourist Office

4 *bis*, place de Samois
77250 Moret-sur-Loing
Tel: (33) 01 60 70 41 66
Fax: (33) 01 60 70 82 52

A small guide available at the Moret tourist office charts the sites where Sisley set up his easel. Many painters continue to live and work in Moret, exhibiting their art at the Moret Salon, Moret Museum, and Pont-Loup Priory. The tourist office also offers guided tours "in Sisley's footsteps" for 40 francs per person. A special tourist package includes a guided tour of the town, an Impressionist picnic with period costumes, and a boat trip along the Loing river on Saturdays, Sundays, and bank holidays from May 1 to October 30.
FEE: 150 francs per person

Cycling, canoeing, and kayaking are also available. Information for these activities is available at the Moret tourist office.

Other attractions include a summer sound and light spectacle chronicling the town's history; a Barley Sugar Museum devoted to the sweets first created by Benedictine nuns in the 17th century, which are still made and sold in Moret; and the Clemenceau House, where Madeleine Clemenceau, the daughter-in-law of Georges Clemenceau, the French statesman and loyal friend of Claude Monet, offers guided tours through the memento-filled family home.

Bourron-Marlotte

This picturesque village, located on the southern border of the Fontainebleau forest in the Loing valley, has attracted many artists and writers. Landscape painters from neighboring Barbizon came here during the mid-nineteenth century, followed by Monet, Sisley, Pissarro, Renoir, and Cézanne, as well as the writers Émile Zola and Théophile Gauthier.

Bourron-Marlotte Tourist Office (Syndicat d'Initiative)

14 *bis*, rue Marechal Foch
77780 Bourron-Marlotte
Tel: (33) 01 64 45 88 86

Vulaines-sur-Seine

Stéphane Mallarmé Museum (Musée Departemental Stéphane Mallarmé)

Pont de Valvins
4, quai Stéphane Mallarmé
77870 Vulaines-sur-Seine
Tel: (33) 01 64 23 73 27

The celebrated 19th-century poet Stéphane Mallarmé, a loyal supporter of the Impressionists and friend of Manet, Degas, Renoir, and Monet, settled in 1874 in Vulaines-sur-Seine, a small village along the banks of the Seine across from the Fontainebleau forest. His simple country home, where he lived until his death in 1898, is now a museum devoted to his life and art. An intimate picture of the artist is conveyed through original furnishings and personal belongings such as Mallarmé's blanket, books, pipes, photographs by Nadar, as well as letters, manuscripts and books of his poems illustrated by André Masson, Ellsworth Kelly, and others. There is also a taped recording of Debussy's *L'Après Midi d'Une Faune*, based on Mallarmé's poem of the same name. He held weekly salons here with his many artist and writer friends.

Provins

The medieval town of Provins is located about 30 miles east of Barbizon. Provins, the former capital of the Counts of Champagne, stages elaborate historical spectacles featuring hundreds of costumed participants, a jousting tournament, and falconry displays. The town also hosts medieval feasts and festivals, a sound and light show, and a potters' market at various times throughout the year. For information, contact the tourist office.

Provins Tourist Office
Cité Médiévale
77160 Provins
Tel: (33) 01 64 60 26 26

Meaux

The medieval city of Meaux, in the heart of brie country about one half hour from Paris, produces an exceptional historical spectacle each year from June to September that is considered to be one of the best in France. Five hundred costumed actors reenact 12 centuries of the city's history, complete with fireworks and a laser light show. Meaux is also known for its ancient episcopal quarter with its important religious buildings and monuments, and a Brie Exhibition Center that traces the history of this popular cheese.

Meaux Tourist Office
2, rue Saint-Rémy
77100 Meaux
Tel: (33) 01 64 33 02 26.

Note: The Seine-et-Marne Tourist Office (listed on p. 75) can provide comprehensive information in English on all of the above-mentioned sites.

Museums in Paris with works by Millet:

Musée d'Orsay
The Angelus
The Gleaners
Musée du Louvre
drawings

Rosa Bonheur: *The Horse Fair*
(1853-55), The Metropolitan
Museum of Art, Gift of
Cornelius Vanderbilt, (1887) (87.25)
Photograph © 1997 The
Metropolitan Museum of Art.

Rosa Bonheur

One of the most successful women artists of all time, Rosa Bonheur gained international fame for her powerful, sympathetic portrayals of animals as well as her independent, eccentric lifestyle. Her work nevertheless fell into obscurity for much of the twentieth century, eclipsed by changing tastes and the modernist revolution. Born in 1822, Bonheur received her artistic training from her father, a painter and member of a utopian socialist movement that advocated equality of the sexes. The family moved to Paris in 1829, where Bonheur attended a progressive coed school. Her mother died when she was eleven, and the loss deeply affected her for the rest of her life. The family of a childhood playmate, Nathalie Micas, informally adopted Bonheur, and Nathalie became her lifelong companion. Bonheur's earliest sketches show a special affinity for animals, which she observed at the zoo at Paris's Jardin des Plantes and among her family's own small menagerie. Having established herself as a leading *animalier*, or animal painter, at the Salon of 1848, Bonheur also drew attention for sketching at the city's slaughterhouses dressed in male clothing—a practice that was not only unconventional but technically illegal at that time. Her greatest success came at the Salon of 1853 with *The Horse Fair*, which attracted both popular and critical acclaim, including the praise of the great Romantic painter Eugène Delacroix. By the end of the 1850s, financially secure and with an international reputation established, Bonheur sought refuge from the cosmopolitan art world. She sold her studio and stable in Paris and settled permanently with Nathalie and her mother in the Château de By near the Fontainebleau forest, just south of Paris.

Anna Klumpke: *Rosa Bonheur* (1898), The Metropolitan Museum of Art, Gift of the artist in memory of Rosa Bonheur, (1922) (22.222) Photograph © 1980 The Metropolitan Museum of Art.

Bonheur in Thomery
1860–1899
Queen of the Beasts

"I made up my mind to 'go to the birds,' to quote Aristophanes," Rosa Bonheur explained to the young American portrait painter Anna Klumpke. "One of my friends, Count d'Armaille, agreed to look for a house for me. It had to be far away from any commotion and so isolated that I could let myself go and live the life of the forest and fields. Close to Fontainebleau he discovered this property. . . . There are about seven and a half acres of land, planted with age-old trees that stand comparison with those of the neighboring forest, and a two-story house that people around here call the château. It was just what I wanted, and I bought it."

Bonheur was at the height of her success in 1859, when she purchased the Château de By in the village of Thomery, about forty miles southeast of Paris. Her monumental painting, *The Horse Fair*, had made her the toast of the French art world, and the English and American collectors were vying for her paintings and engravings. Many artists and society figures frequented her Paris home and studio on the rue d'Assas, which also attracted admirers seeking her autograph. "If I hadn't upped and decided to seek exile in the Fontainebleau forest, in no time flat they would have made it impossible for me to go on working," the commanding Bonheur good-naturedly lamented.

The centuries-old stone and red brick Château de By and the adjoining high-towered studio that Bonheur added upon her arrival are an imposing presence among the simple, shuttered stone houses and ivy-draped walls of this small village. Bonheur lovingly dubbed her new residence "The Domain of Perfect Affection."

In 1860, she set up house here along with her companion, Nathalie Micas, and Micas's mother, whose love and support nurtured her artistic development. These two women oversaw

In Bonheur's studio in the Château de By (opposite), a large brass chandelier hangs above heavily carved cabinets; imposing, Gothic-style chairs with tassled, embroidered seat covers; and shelves of books on topics ranging from natural history and travel to English literature.

Bonheur's house and studio in the tiny village of By were a refuge from the demanding social life she led as a celebrity in Paris.

all domestic matters so that Bonheur could paint her animals in peace. Nathalie, an artist herself and inventor of a railroad brake, also prepared her friend's canvases, acted as a tough liaison with Bonheur's art dealers, and jealously guarded their privacy.

Bonheur's other trusted companions, her animals, occupied a small farm and stables behind the château. "I fenced in the lot next door and built some little sheds, sparing nothing for my animals' comfort," Bonheur noted. "At times this place has been a veritable Noah's ark: mouflons, stags, does, izards (sic), boars, sheep, horses, oxen, and even lions. I was very fond of all my boarders, the sheep most of all."

Today, a Scottish bullock horn hanging from a chain sounds a bell at the iron gate leading to Bonheur's studio, which has been meticulously restored and opened to the public. The walls of the entry hall are stamped with Bonheur's initials and mounted with antique swords, rams' horns, a horse head, and riding crops. The overall effect recalls the historic hunting lodges of French kings. Surely, no ordinary woman resided here.

In the cavernous studio, defined by a soaring wood-beamed ceiling, columned stone walls, and parquet floors, Bonheur's uncompromising life is evoked by her many possessions, paintings, and sketches, displayed exactly as the artist left them.

"I call the studio my sanctuary because everything there reminds me of something dear to my heart," said Bonheur. "The horns and antlers up on the walls adorned the sheep, stags, and oxen who used to pose for me. These animals lived with me as my friends, and I drew them over and over."

Her painting, *Race of Wild Horses*, still rests unfinished on her easel. On the small wooden table next to it lie her worn palettes and a jar of paintbrushes. Also on display is an illuminated slide of *The Horse Fair*, purchased in 1887 by the American tycoon Cornelius Vanderbilt.

Among the most illustrious visitors to her studio was Empress Eugènie, wife of Napoleon III, who presented her with the Legion of Honor in 1865, remarking that "genius has no sex." Bonheur was the first woman artist to receive France's highest accolade.

A portrait of Bonheur by Anna Klumpke occupies another large easel. Dressed in her blue painter's smock and holding her palette and brushes, Bonheur poses with characteristic confidence in front of a work in progress. Her short-cropped gray hair frames her broad forehead and sparkling black eyes. "I prayed God to let me capture the penetrating gaze and the benevolent, poetic air that emanated from her whole person," wrote Klumpke about her struggle to evoke her friend's singular personality in a portrait. The strong-willed Bonheur was not exactly an accommodating model, having delayed and distracted Klumpke to the point of frustration, a tactic that served to prolong her enjoyable visits with the young American portraitist. Klumpke, for her part, was enchanted by Bonheur's "rich and diverse mind," her knowledge of music, literature, and art, and her "spirited, offhand conversation."

Dubbed the Diana of Fontainebleau by local residents who compared her to the Greek goddess of the hunt, Bonheur defied convention by riding her horses astride instead of

On Bonheur's desk, built low to the ground to accommodate the artist's short stature, rest her eyeglasses, a small travel journal, a bronze inkwell, and a vase of feathers plucked from some of the more than sixty birds that she kept in gilded cages in her bedroom.

sidesaddle through the forest. "I'd go off at sunrise with my paint box on my back, dogs trailing behind and gun in hand, ready to shoot any game I might see," recalled Bonheur.

Bonheur was legendary not only for her artistic accomplishments but also for her shocking custom of often dressing in masculine attire. As a young woman she began wearing men's clothes for comfort and practicality on her outings to sketch in the open air. "Trousers have been my great protectors . . . I've often felt proud to have dared break with traditions that would have made me drag skirts everywhere, making it impossible for me to do certain kinds of work," Bonheur explained.

Arranged on the Gothic-style chair is Bonheur's satchel of painting supplies, used on her frequent jaunts in the forest. Here, too, are her khaki riding hat, a black velvet jacket, laced high-top shoes, and the blue smock she often wore with peasant trousers while painting.

Men's clothing also served as a protective disguise in the crude, male-dominated world of the slaughterhouses and horse fairs, where Bonheur went to draw animals from life, sometimes even carrying a pistol.

In 19th-century France it was illegal for women to wear men's clothes in public. Offenders risked arrest, fines, and even prison terms. Women who insisted upon trousers were required to obtain special permission from the police. A copy of one of Bonheur's cross-dressing permits is on display in her studio. This law, which still exists, was more frequently enforced during times of feminist agitation.

She credited her father with fostering her feminist ideals:

Rosa Bonheur: *Col. William F. Cody* (1889), Buffalo Bill Historical Center, Cody, WY; given in memory of William R. Coe and Mai Rogers Coe.

"To his doctrines I owe my great and glorious ambition for the sex to which I proudly belong, whose independence I'll defend till my dying day." The artist made no secret of her aversion to marriage, insisting, "Our timid beauties of old Europe are too easily led to the altar, like ewes going to sacrifice in pagan temples." She went on, "A long time ago I understood that when a girl dons a crown of orange blossoms, she becomes subordinate, nothing but a pale reflection of what she was before. She's forever the leader's companion, not his equal, but his helpmate."

Bonheur's tranquil routine at By was disrupted in 1870 with the outbreak of the Franco-Prussian War. Seeing herself as a modern Joan of Arc, she mobilized local citizens for battle. Ultimately restrained by the mayor of Thomery, she and Nathalie had to limit their contribution to the war effort to making soup for the locals.

After France's defeat, Bonheur became interested in wild

The beaded and leather Indian costume displayed in the glass cabinet in the studio hallway was a gift to the artist from Buffalo Bill.

cats, sketching lions and panthers at Paris's circuses and at the Jardin des Plantes. For a time, she lived with three of her own lions who proved to be "rather cumbersome, expensive boarders" who required twenty pounds of beef each day. One of Bonheur's engravings of her felines rests on the easel next to her portrait.

Bonheur was equally fascinated with all things American, particularly the West and its Native Americans, whom she observed firsthand at Buffalo Bill Cody's Wild West Show at the Universal Exposition in Paris in 1889. Cody, the flamboyant American showman, Pony Express rider, and Indian fighter, staged a hugely successful spectacle there, filled with wild animals, displays of horsemanship, and reenactments of

Indian attacks and episodes from American history. The show fired Bonheur's romantic imagination. Grief-stricken by the death that year of her beloved Nathalie, she found an invigorating diversion at Cody's campsite, where she made numerous studies for paintings of cowboys, Indians, bison, and mustangs.

Cody and Bonheur, both masters of self-promotion, became instant friends. "Buffalo Bill was extremely good to me," recalled Bonheur. "He was nice as could be about letting me work among his redskins every day. That gave me time to study their tents; I watched everything they did, and talked as best I could with the warriors. Observing them at close range really refreshed my sad old mind."

At By, Bonheur painted an equestrian portrait of Cody, which was widely reproduced on posters and postcards. Cody sent the portrait back to America, where it is now part of the collection of the Buffalo Bill Historical Center in Cody, Wyoming. That same year, a chance meeting with the thirty-three-year-old American painter Anna Klumpke led to an intimate relationship that sustained Bonheur in her last years. Klumpke, whom Bonheur affectionately called a "sister of the brush," first came to By as an interpreter for an American rancher who had sent Bonheur a mustang. She visited regularly from 1895 onward, and settled there permanently in 1898. Almost immediately, the two artists began construction of a larger, skylit studio opposite the original one. But they were to have very little time there together. Bonheur died the next year, at age seventy-seven, after a brief bout with pulmonary influenza.

Her mahogany deathbed dominates the study adjacent to her studio. Here, more than a century later, a host of personal memorabilia, including sketches and paintings by Bonheur, photo albums, initialed linen handkerchiefs and envelopes, a stuffed parrot, and a wardrobe filled with clothes, vividly recall her dynamic presence. A mannequin of the artist reposes in an armchair, wearing a long green dress and black jacket decorated with her Legion of Honor medal.

"The morning of the funeral I wanted a moment alone underneath the great oaks that had been Rosa Bonheur's pride

and joy," reflected Klumpke, who inherited most of Bonheur's estate. "Her coffin left in a white-draped hearse through the main entrance, with the iron gates thrown open wide."

After her funeral in the church in Thomery, Bonheur was buried in Paris's Père Lachaise cemetery alongside Nathalie, with many friends and artists present at her graveside. The inscription on her tomb reads: "Friendship is a Divine Affection." Anna Klumpke's ashes joined them there in 1945.

NOTE: Many of Bonheur's quotes are from Anna Klumpke's book, *Rosa Bonheur: The Artist's (Auto) Biography*, in which Klumpke transcribed conversations with the artist.

The overall effect of Bonheur's studio recalls the historic hunting lodges of French kings.

Thomery

Rosa Bonheur's home and studio can be found in the hamlet of By in the picturesque village of Thomery about twelve miles from Barbizon. Thomery is known for its production of sweet grapes known as chasselas, whose vines drape the village's stone walls.

✵ How To Get There

By Car
The region is best toured by car. Rental agencies are listed under Fontainebleau (page 75).

By Train
Tel: (33) 08 36 35 35 39
Trains from Paris's Gare de Lyon stop at Thomery (about a 45-minute ride). Bonheur's home and studio are about a 20-minute walk from the Thomery station, through the Fontainebleau forest. Signs point in the direction of By. Since Thomery is a small village, taxis are rarely available at the train station. A more convenient option is to take the train from the Gare de Lyon (Banlieu line) to Fontainebleau-Avon (about a 40-minute ride, 94 francs round trip), and then take a taxi from the station to nearby Thomery.

Taxis
Fontainebleau to Thomery
Tel: (33) 06 09 93 63 77
The trip is about 3 miles; one-way fare is about 70 francs.

✵ Tourist Office

Thomery Tourist Office
11, rue de la République
77810 Thomery.
Tel: (33) 01 64 70 81 14
HOURS: Open Wednesday and Saturday only, 10 a.m. to 12 p.m. and 3 p.m. to 5:30 p.m., from April 1 to October 31.

✵ House and Studio of Rosa Bonheur

Château de By
12, rue Rosa Bonheur
77810 Thomery
Tel: (33) 01 60 70 04 49
HOURS: open Wednesdays and Saturdays from 2 p.m. to 5 p.m.
ENTRY FEE: 15 francs; 10 francs for children, senior citizens, and groups of 10 or more.

✵ Dining and Accommodations

Hostellerie le Vieux Logis
5, rue Sadi Carnot
77810 Thomery
Tel: (33) 01 60 96 44 77
Fax: (33) 01 60 70 01 42
This three-star property, housed in an 18th-century home, offers fourteen spacious, modern rooms (400 francs) and an elegant dining room (open for lunch and dinner), garden terrace, and swimming pool. The fine cuisine includes grilled fish, roast lamb, filet of beef, grilled duck, oysters, cheeses, and desserts. Menus are priced at 155 francs and 240 francs; à la carte items range from 55 francs to 155 francs.

Museums in Paris with works by Bonheur:

✵ Musée d'Orsay
Plowing in the Nivernais

A spiral staircase adds a touch of
Renaissance drama to the large
entrance hall in Rosa Bonheur's
home.

Gustave Courbet: *La Grotte de la
Loue* (c. 1865), National Gallery of
Art, Washington, D. C., gift of
Charles L. Lindemann.

Gustave Courbet

Not only did Gustave Courbet's Realist paintings alienate the Parisian art world, his radical politics ultimately led to political imprisonment and subsequent exile. The son of a well-to-do farming family, he was born in 1819 in the small town of Ornans. At twenty, he moved to Paris, eventually realizing his vocation to paint. Uninspired by academic teaching, he enrolled in the more liberal Académie Suisse, which later attracted Pissarro and Monet. He immersed himself in bohemian life, frequenting cafes, and gaining a reputation as a lover of beer, music, and women. He formed close friendships with a politically charged group of artists, writers, and intellectuals, who, in the wake of the Revolution of 1848, became the core of the movement known as Realism. While Courbet did not participate in the actual fighting, he and his contemporaries waged an intellectual war through their pointedly democratic writings and art, which portrayed social classes and activities previously considered unworthy of representation, thereby serving as agents of social reform. His first major success, *After Dinner at Ornans*, was awarded a second-prize medal at the Salon of 1849, where it was acclaimed by Delacroix and purchased by the State. Over the next three decades, drawing upon his rural roots for nourishment and inspiration, he fell in and out of political favor, all the while producing some of the most powerful artistic statements of his time and establishing himself as a visionary pioneer of the avant-garde.

Portrait of Gustave Courbet, Bibliothèque Nationale de France, Paris.

Courbet in Ornans
1849–1873
Master Painter

"There are a lot of idiots who think that you can do a landscape just like that! . . . Well, that's just a joke! To paint a country, you have to know it. I know my country and I paint it. Those bushes, they're from where I live; that river, that's the Loue, and this one is the Lison; those rocks are from Ornans and the Black Well. Go and see, and you'll recognize all my pictures," Gustave Courbet proclaimed.

Courbet returned from Paris to his native Ornans in 1849, exhilarated by the Salon success of his painting, *After Dinner at Ornans*. Unfazed by one critic's attack that "no one could drag art into the gutter with greater technical virtuosity," he defended his representation of common people and declared that "art must be dragged into the gutter!" Courbet's painterly expression of that belief brought him a relentless storm of hostility and negative criticism.

It was to Ornans, a small country town on the Loue River in southeastern France, that he would return again and again in the years to come, drawing comfort from his cherished family and from the majestic landscape he had grown to love as a child. Today, its beauty remains undiminished.

The sleepy town of Ornans survives virtually unchanged since Courbet's time. Its centuries-old houses overhanging the Loue, the 12th-century church with its elegant belfry, the stone bridges, old mills, and the Roche du Mont—a rugged cliff that rises behind the town like a fortress—appear in many of his paintings.

The simple 18th-century stone townhouse where Courbet was born hugs the bank of the Loue with a quiet dignity, its reflection shimmering in the river. Now a museum dedicated to the artist's life and furnished from the period, it houses more than sixty works by Courbet, his friends, and followers, as well as by 20th-century artists who have been inspired by

Courbet's many trips home to Ornans were a source of inspiration and renewal. The jagged rocks and forests, hidden ravines, waterfalls, and streams of his native Franche-Comté (opposite) were the painter's refuge against the stresses of Paris and the authoritarian regime of Napoleon III. His several versions of *The Source of the Loue River* and *The Brook of the Black Well* reveal a majestic nature as a place of harmony and freedom. When asked how he painted such beautiful landscapes, Courbet replied: "I feel it."

the region. Courbet also spent part of his childhood at his father's farm in the neighboring village of Flagey. The farmhouse, although abandoned, is still intact, situated along a country road just beyond the village church and marked by a modest plaque near the arched entrance.

Courbet's father was a prosperous landowner and farmer possessed of both peasant and bourgeois loyalties. His maternal grandfather, a committed leftist and supporter of the French Revolution, infused the young Courbet with a spirit of independence, advising him to "shout loudly and march straight." In the years to come, Courbet never failed to heed that advice.

Courbet was the adored eldest son in a close, supportive family. In a household devoted to camaraderie and simple country pleasures, he often joined his family as they listened to poems or sang folksongs in the evening, accompanied by a violinist friend. "I cannot help but feel that this warm environment of tender feelings, of primitive art and folk poetry, in which Courbet passed his youth, has contributed a great deal to the development of his thought. The egg of 'Realism' came out

The 18th-century stone townhouse where Courbet was born is now a museum dedicated to his life and art. Period antiques and clothing adorn the second-floor birth room (opposite).

In the wood-panelled sitting room of Courbet's house, red velvet armchairs and a neoclassical secretary create an atmosphere of middle-class respectability. The convivial Courbet family frequently gathered here for songs in the evening.

of this nest," wrote Jules-Antoine Castagnary, a liberal politician and art critic who was one of Courbet's closest supporters.

But Courbet was more than a country rustic. In Paris, he proclaimed his own greatness at every opportunity, presenting himself as an uncivilized bohemian, anarchist, and socialist. His noisy self-confidence and outspoken manner both irritated and engaged his contemporaries, according to Théophile Silvestre, an art critic and habitué of the Brasserie Andler, where Courbet, Baudelaire, Daumier, and other friends often gathered. "Courbet is all integrity and good nature," Silvestre wrote. "His love for the cafe and his noctambulant habits damage his talent . . . He is sometimes witty, always bizarre . . . His bearing is low-class; his body bends over a oaken stick or a vine-stock with a curved handle–a prop, which, like his cheesemonger's pipe that is always lit, never leaves him . . . His dress bespeaks a simple man, well-to-do, and not without affectation."

Courbet established his reputation with three works depicting peasants, laborers, and rural townspeople that were

exhibited in Paris at the Salon of 1850–51. *The Stonebreakers, A Burial at Ornans,* and *The Peasants of Flagey Returning from the Fair* were painted in Ornans and inspired by Courbet's country origins, portraying for the first time on a heroic scale the lives of peasants. Executed in a style that was rooted in the 17th-century Dutch and Spanish masters and popular imagery like folk art and woodcut prints, these works are distinguished by their austerity and directness. Courbet's unidealized subject matter, which suggested the inevitable rise of the working class, and his stark, honest style offended both conservative critics and the bourgeois public alike.

Courbet's landmark painting *A Burial at Ornans,* which is thought to be based on the funeral of his great-uncle, further demonstrates the link between his art and leftist politics. Revolutionary in style, size, and subject, the canvas depicts fifty life-size figures representing Courbet's family, friends, and villagers gathered at a graveside in the Ornans cemetery. The public was shocked not only by the painting's lack of spiritual and narrative meaning but by Courbet's portrayal

Gustave Courbet: *After Dinner at Ornans* (1848–49), Musée des Beaux-Arts, Lille; Giraudon/Art Resource, New York.

of the death of a common man on a scale befitting historical subjects. Even the townspeople of Ornans felt slighted by what they considered to be caricatures of themselves.

Courbet's modern history paintings had made him famous by the age of thirty-one. The artist welcomed the fame, as well as the uproar surrounding his work. "When I am no longer controversial I will no longer be important," he declared.

At the house in Ornans, a small entrance hall leads into the kitchen and dining area, where a simple wooden table and large stone fireplace recall the shadowy, rustic atmosphere of *After Dinner at Ornans*. Displayed in the adjacent sitting room are photographs of the artist in his studio, a sculpted likeness, and a sketch by Édouard Manet of Courbet smoking his clay pipe, which is also preserved here. Courbet is shown with a full beard and what he himself called an "Assyrian profile." "The really wonderful thing about his face, which was like the mask of an Assyrian idol with an added element of village rusticity, was the look in his eyes: two eyes, no, two lakes, wide, deep, soft and blue," according to the caricaturist André Gill.

In the adjoining exhibition room are displayed a painter's stool, walking stick, palette, paintbrushes, and palette knives that Courbet used to such powerful effect in masterpieces such as his monumental autobiographical painting, *The Studio of the Painter: A Real Allegory Determining Seven Years of My Life as an Artist* (1855), in which Courbet depicts himself painting a landscape from his home region, surrounded by figures from various strata of society. He was also noted for his sensuous nudes, landscapes, and hunting scenes.

During the late 1850s and 1860s, Courbet produced images that were less overtly political. His leftist views resurfaced, however, in his anticlerical works of the 1860s. In the last exhibition space on the first floor of the Courbet Museum there is a study for *The Return from the Conference*, a satirical painting of drunken priests after one of their weekly dinners near Ornans. The painting, seen as a critique of religious ideology, was later purchased and destroyed by some of those it offended. Among the other works on display here are Courbet's engravings, anticlerical pamphlets illus-

In the second-floor room where Courbet was born, a small wooden cradle and bed, a spinning wheel, two secretaries, a marble-topped washstand, and period clothing create the look of an inhabited 19th-century interior.

trated with his drawings, and a photograph of the writer and socialist philosopher Pierre-Joseph Proudhon.

Elsewhere in the house, furnishings from the period are accompanied by a portrait and photograph of the artist, portraits of friends and family, regional landscapes, snowscapes, and several semi-impressionistic seascapes executed in his later years.

In the third-floor attic are photos of Courbet in his studio and painting outside under an umbrella; works of other landscape painters from Franche-Comté; a reproduction of Courbet's masterpiece, *The Studio of the Painter*; and a plaster model of his sculpture, *Fisherman of Chavots*, a bronze copy

Gustave Courbet: *A Burial at Ornans: Historical Painting* (1849), Musée d'Orsay, Paris; photo © Erich Lessing, Art Resource, New York.

of which now stands in the place Courbet in Ornans.

Courbet's long stays in Franche-Comté during the 1860s may have been partly motivated by his uncompromising political positions, sometimes in favor, often out of favor, with various ruling parties. While serving as a fine arts delegate under the short-lived socialist government of the Paris Commune in 1871, Courbet was accused of participating in the infamous destruction of the Vendôme Column in Paris. He was arrested, fined, and jailed. A self-portrait in the sitting room was painted while serving his six-month sentence at St. Pélagie prison in Paris.

After prison, Courbet met with hostility in both Paris and Ornans, where his studio had been looted by the Prussians and vandalized by locals. Compounding his troubles, the government passed a law in 1873 that held Courbet financially responsible for the reconstruction of the Vendôme Column, requiring him to pay a huge sum of more than 300 thousand francs. Excluded from the Salons, with his property confiscated, the beleaguered artist took refuge in Switzerland in 1873.

He continued to paint landscapes in his new surroundings, including *Le Château de Chillon*, exhibited on the second floor of the Courbet home. In an effort to raise enough money to pay for restoration of the column and return to France, Courbet worked feverishly with the help of assistants, and was even accused of signing some of their paintings to augment their value. Depressed and overburdened by financial worries, he continued to drink heavily despite deteriorating health. Stricken by dropsy, Courbet died, exhausted, in 1877, at La Tour-de-Peilz in Switzerland at the age of fifty-eight.

The exile's body was returned to his home in Ornans. Far up on the hill behind the church, Courbet was buried in the local cemetery beneath a tall rock that appears to have tumbled out of one of his paintings, solidly reaffirming the visionary courage and earthy grandeur of the master painter from Ornans.

Ornans

Ornans is about 250 miles southeast of Paris. It is located in the Loue valley in the department of Doubs in the Franche-Comté region of France, near the Swiss border. Early settlers were attracted to the fertile slopes of the Loue River valley, which were once covered with vineyards. Along rue Édouard Bastide in Ornans are 16th- and 17th-century vine-growers' houses with their typical arched doors. Most of the buildings date from the 16th to 18th centuries. Traversed by 17th-century stone bridges and studded with old water and saw mills, the Loue was once the lifeline of Ornans. Known for its excellent trout, the Loue's calm, shallow waters are considered one of the best rivers for fly fishing in France.

☙ How To Get There

By Car
Ornans is approximately a 4½ hour drive from Paris. Take autoroute A6 (direction Lyon) to Beaune. From Beaune, take autoroute A31 (direction Dijon) for about two miles, and then the A36 highway to Besançon. In Besançon, take road N57 for about 2 miles, and then road D67 to Ornans.

By Train
Tel: (33) 08 36 35 35 39
TGV trains depart daily from Paris's Gare de Lyon station to Besançon, a city about sixteen miles from Ornans. The ride through wheat and sunflower fields, rolling hills, and pastures takes about 2½ hours. Round trip fare is 514 francs. Tickets should be purchased at the windows marked Grandes Lignes. Don't forget to validate (*composter*) your ticket at the orange post-like structures located throughout the train stations (often near the tracks). Failure to do so will result in a fine from train inspectors on board.

Taxis
Taxis Ornans (to Besançon)
Tel: (33) 03 81 62 16 79
Taxis Besançon (to Ornans)
Tel: (33) 03 81 88 80 80
Taxis that will take you to Ornans are usually waiting at the Besçanon station. However, the 20-minute ride is about 194 francs one way.

Buses
Tel: (33) 03 81 21 22 00
A more economical option are the buses that travel between Besançon and Ornans. Ask for a schedule at the train station or at the Ornans tourist office. The 40-minute ride is about 42 francs round trip.

Car Rentals
The train stop for Ornans, Besançon, is also a good place to rent a car for exploring the countryside around Ornans.

Avis
7, place Flore
25000 Besançon
Tel: (33) 03 81 80 91 08

Hertz
3, place Flore
25000 Besançon
Tel: (33) 03 81 47 43 23

Bicycle Rentals
Cycle du Val
6, rue Pierre Vernier
Ornans
Tel: (33) 03 81 57 18 08
It is possible to tour Ornans by bicycle or mountain bike, which can be rented for 100 francs per day.

☙ Tourist Office

Besançon Tourist Office
2, Place de la 1er Armée Francaise
25000 Besançon
Tel: (33) 03 81 80 92 55

Ornans Tourist Office (Office du Tourisme Syndicat d'Initiative)
7, rue Pierre Vernier
25290 Ornans
Tel/Fax: (33) 03 81 62 21 50
The tourist office offers free brochures and maps of Ornans and the surrounding countryside. Guided tours of Ornans are available in English for groups of 10 or more for 300 francs. Reserve in advance by written request.
HOURS: Open Monday through Saturday from 9:30 a.m. to 12 p.m. and 2 p.m. to 6 p.m.

☙ House and Studio of Gustave Courbet

Musée Gustave Courbet
(The painter's birthplace)
1, place Robert Fernier
25290 Ornans
Tel: (33) 03 81 62 23 30
The 18th-century stone townhouse where Courbet was born in 1819 is now a museum. Behind the Courbet home, an exhibition space displays photographs tracing the life and work of Courbet, as well as reproductions of some of his works, including *A Burial at Ornans* (1849–50).
HOURS: The museum is open all year from 10 a.m. to 12 p.m. and 2 p.m. to 6 p.m. Open from 10 a.m. to 6 p.m. July and August. Closed Tuesdays from November 1 to March 31. Closed May 1, Christmas day and Easter day.
ENTRY FEE: 20 francs; 15 francs per person for groups; 10 francs for children and students.

♣ Ornans Sites

The sleepy, picturesque town of Ornans (population 4,200) is a virtual open-air museum of Courbet's paintings. He captured the reflections of the old stone and wood houses crowded along the banks of the Loue River in his painting *Le Miroir d'Ornans* (1872), displayed in the Musée Courbet. A reproduction rests on an easel adjacent to the de Gaulle bridge near the center of town. One of Courbet's earliest landscapes, *Le Pont de Nahin à Ornans* (1837), a view of the old Nahin bridge off rue Édouard Bastide, is on display in the Musée Courbet. The Roche du Mont, the signature limestone cliff that rises above Ornans, provided the backdrop for Courbet's celebrated painting, *A Burial at Ornans*, as well as several landscapes.

Château of Ornans

The Château of Ornans, which appears in several of Courbet's paintings, no longer exists, but the name is now used for the rock formation overlooking the Loue valley. Several houses now occupy the former site of a 12th-century citadel that was destroyed by Louis XIV to suppress local resistance to central authority. In *Le Château d'Ornans* (1854–55), painted while the authoritarian Napoleon III was in power, Courbet proudly refers to the independent past of his region. Best viewed from the grounds of the Ornans church, this site can be reached via rue du Château. It is marked by a reproduction of Courbet's painting, now in the Minneapolis Institute of Arts.

Church and Cemetery of Ornans

In the cemetery of the 12th-century Saint-Laurent church, situated on the riverbank at the center of town, an iron cross marks the tomb of Benjamin Bonnet (1803–1865), the pastor represented in Courbet's *A Burial at Ornans*.

Courbet's Grave

Although Courbet was initially interred in Switzerland, where he died in 1877, his body was returned to Ornans in 1919 to the very cemetery that had been the setting for his *A Burial at Ornans*. It is located off rue de Chantrans on the hill behind the church; a modest rock inscribed with Courbet's signature serves as his gravestone.

Courbet's Studio

The studio where Courbet painted *A Burial at Ornans* is located at #24 place Gustave Courbet in the center of town. The studio was in the attic of his late grandfather's house. A lantern hangs from the side of the beige stucco structure, which is accented with light blue shutters. The citizens of Ornans came here to pose for the painting, but Courbet complained that the studio was so small that he couldn't back up sufficiently to inspect his canvas. This may explain the "additive" look of his composition, in which the figures appear to be clumped together in a collage-like fashion. Courbet also had another studio in Ornans, located at the Rond Point de l'Europe along the main road to Besançon. Formerly known as Le Chalet, it is now a wine merchant's house called Maison Marguier.

Fisherman of Chavots

At the fountain in place Gustave Courbet is a bronze copy of Courbet's *Fisherman of Chavots* (1862), a sculpture of a nude boy fishing with a trident that Courbet had made at his short-lived teaching studio on rue Notre-Dame-des-Champs in Paris. (Chavot is a type of fish found in the Loue.) He donated the piece to the town of Ornans for one of its public fountains. In 1871, after the events of the Paris Commune brought nationwide discredit to Courbet, the Town

The violin displayed in Courbet's home recalls the convivial atmosphere in which the painter grew up. His family often sang folk songs in the evening, accompanied by a violinist friend.

Council deemed the sculpture indecent and had it removed. It was later replaced by a second cast that Courbet had entrusted to a friend. That sculpture was vandalized in 1909, and a restoration is in progress.

Place Gustave Courbet is also the site of a lively outdoor market which takes place on the third Tuesday of each month. Cheeses, sausage, honey, and other products from the region are for sale, as well as clothing and souvenirs.

❧ Dining

Le France
51-53, rue Pierre Vernier
25290 Ornans
Tel: (33) 03 81 62 24 44
Fax: (33) 03 81 62 12 03
This three-star restaurant in the Hôtel de France is the finest in Ornans. Menus ranging from 150 francs to 310 francs offer foie gras, roast pigeon, filet mignon, lamb, grilled salmon, and regional specialties such as filet of trout, morel mushrooms, and Comté cheese.
HOURS: Lunch is served from 12 p.m. to 1:30 p.m; dinner is served from 7:30 p.m. to 9 p.m.

Lighter fare is available in the brasserie.
HOURS: Breakfast from 7:30 a.m. to 10 a.m., lunch from 12 p.m. to 2 p.m., dinner from 7 p.m. to 9 p.m. Menus are 80 francs and 100 francs.

Le Progrès
11, rue Jacques Gervais
25290 Ornans
Tel: (33) 03 81 62 16 79
Fax: (33) 03 81 62 19 10
The restaurant of the Hotel Le Progrès offers menus ranging from 98 francs to 170 francs. Dishes include trout, filet of perch, smoked ham, regional sausage, salads, and fresh vegetable plates.
HOURS: 7 a.m. to 10 p.m.; closed Sunday evenings.

Restaurant Le Courbet
34, rue Pierre Vernier
25290 Ornans
Tel: (33) 03 81 62 10 15
This charming restaurant across the street from Hôtel de France serves a 150 franc menu featuring trout with Chardonnay, lamb, melon soup, and regional cheeses. Pastries, ice cream, and drinks are served on the outdoor terrace every afternoon.
HOURS: Open every day but Tuesday, 12 p.m. to 2:30 p.m. and 7 p.m. to 9:30 p.m.

Le Dolmen/Le Sainte Anne
52, 54, 56, rue Pierre Vernier
25290 Ornans
Tel: (33) 03 81 62 13 70
This restaurant, crèperie, and tea salon at place Robert Humblot has a large, tree-shaded outdoor terrace offering a scenic view of the Loue River and the back of Courbet's home. One of the best places to stop for a quick bite while touring the town, Le Dolmen/Le Sainte Anne offers reasonably priced salads, crèpes, omelets, fresh fish, and a large selection of ice cream. Menus range from 88 francs to 138 francs.
HOURS: Open every day but Monday from 10 a.m. to midnight. Closed for the month of October.

Cafe du Pêcheur
Place Gustave Courbet
25290 Ornans
Tel: (33) 03 81 57 19 95
Named after Courbet's sculpture Fisherman of Chavots, a replica of which stands at the fountain in the square, this cafe and bar serves salads, local trout and perch, grilled meats, pizza, and sandwiches. The rustic interior has rush-seated chairs and a wood-beamed ceiling. Dining is also available outside on the covered porch overlooking the square.
HOURS: Open every day from 7:30 a.m. to 1 a.m.

❧ Accommodations

Hôtel de France
51–53, rue Pierre Vernier
25290 Ornans
Tel: (33) 03 81 62 24 44
Fax: (33) 03 81 62 12 03
The nicest hotel in Ornans, the three-star Hôtel de France is housed in a lovely 16th-century building on the main street, just steps away from the Musée Courbet. Several of its 31 rooms, decorated with eclectic vintage furniture, overlook a garden terrace with views of the Roche du Mont and the church of Ornans. Rates are 210 francs (with shower) and 300 francs (with bath) for singles; 300 to 450 francs for doubles; and 350 francs to 480 francs for triples. All rooms have toilets. Breakfast is 45 francs extra, and can be served in the room. Special packages are available for fly fishing enthusiasts. The hotel has a bar/brasserie and a fine dining room. Courbet came here often to meet friends.

Hôtel de la Vallée
39, avenue Wilson
25290 Ornans
Tel: (33) 03 81 62 40 43
This new two-star hotel was built by the owners of Hôtel de France. Seventeen simple but comfortable rooms range in price from 260 francs for a single (with shower) to 310-360 francs (with shower) for a double. Each room has its own toilet. Several rooms overlook the Loue River. Breakfast (40 francs) is available but not included in the price. There is no restaurant on the premises.

Hôtel Le Progrès
11, rue Jacques Gervais
25290 Ornans
Tel: (33) 03 81 62 16 79
Fax: (33) 03 81 62 19 10
This two-star hotel has 15 clean, modest rooms, a bar, restaurant, and tea salon. All rooms have their

own showers and toilets. Prices range from 225 francs to 250 francs for singles; 255 francs to 300 francs for doubles; and 300 francs to 330 francs for triples. Breakfast is 32 francs.

♣ Short Excursions

Around Ornans

Ornans is located in the department of Doubs in the heart of Franche-Comté. Bordered on the east by the Jura mountains, which form a natural frontier with Switzerland, the region of Franche-Comté is noted for its lush natural beauty. Courbet made many painting pilgrimages throughout the Doubs, drawing endless inspiration from its sparkling rivers and lakes, forests, limestone cliffs, springs, and waterfalls. The sites of many of his paintings, marked by easels bearing reproductions, are easily accessible by car (rentals available in Besançon). The Ornans tourist office provides an illustrated map of places such as the source of the Loue River (near the village of Ouhans) and the source of the Lison River (near the village of Nans-sous-Sainte-Anne), both of which flow out of beautiful rock chasms. Other places of interest where Courbet set up his easel include Scey-Maisières (*Countryside Near Maisières*, 1865), Cléron (*Towing on the Bank of the Loue*, 1863, which is exhibited at the Musée Courbet), and the Brême River valley (*The Brook of the Black Well*, 1855).

The breathtaking drive through the countryside offers views of pristine forests, sprawling pastures and farmland, old stone farmhouses, grazing cows and horses, and centuries-old castles and churches.

France's greenest department is known for its rich farming tradition and local products such as Comté cheese (which has a special label of origin), morel mushrooms, Morteau sausage, and fresh river trout and perch cooked in the region's unique yellow wine. The Doubs is also a center of French clockmaking and the birthplace of Peugeot cars.

Attractions range from castles and churches to caves, underground glaciers and waterfalls, and museums devoted to angling (Ornans), wine and vineyards (Lods), cheesemaking (Trepot), and regional costumes (Montgesoye). Dole, another Doubs town and the birthplace of the noted scientist Louis Pasteur, is home to the Pasteur Museum. There is also a fascinating open-air museum of Franche-Comté houses in Nancray, about 10 miles from Besançon. Leisure activities include riverboat cruises, fishing, kayaking, and canoeing on the Loue. The Ornans tourist office can provide further information.

Flagey

Another Courbet family home where the artist spent much of his childhood is located in the small village of Flagey, about seven miles from Ornans. This rustic 18th century farmhouse was purchased by the village and is currently uninhabited. It is situated just up the road from the village church. Flagey retains much of its primitive charm. Even today there is no running water or electricity in some homes.

Besançon

The city of Besançon was transformed into a walled stronghold with a Citadel by Louis XIV's military architect Vauban. Courbet attended boarding school here at the age of 18, before leaving for Paris two years later to become a painter.

Musée des Beaux Arts
Place de la Revolution
Besançon
Tel: (33) 03 81 82 39 89
The museum contains an exceptional collection of paintings by Courbet, Ingres, Titian, Constable, Matisse, Picasso, and others. Among Courbet's works are *The Peasants of Flagey Returning from the Fair*.

Museums in Paris with works by Courbet:

♣ **Musée d'Orsay**
   A Burial at Ornans
   The Studio of the Painter
♣ **Musée du Petit Palais**
   The Young Ladies of the Banks of the Seine

Eugène Delacroix: *The Lion Hunt*
(1860-61), Art Institute of Chicago,
Potter Palmer Collection; photo ©
2000 The Art Institute of Chicago.

Eugène Delacroix

Described by Charles Baudelaire as "the most original painter of ancient or modern times," Eugène Delacroix was the last old master in the tradition of Rembrandt, Titian, and Rubens, and the preeminent painter of French Romanticism, which emphasized the primacy of the artist's inner vision and emotions. Delacroix embodied the contradiction between the revolutionary and the conventional that characterized his time. Skeptical of progress, he painted subjects from history, mythology, and religion like his forefathers, yet his passionate, color-infused style had a profound impact on later artists. Delacroix was born in 1798 near Paris to the daughter of the cabinetmaker to King Louis XV and a cosmopolitan lawyer active in the French Revolution. It has long been rumored, however, that Delacroix's true father was the brilliant statesman Talleyrand, to whom he bore a striking resemblance. His debut painting, *The Barque of Dante,* shown at the Salon of 1822, was an instant success. Nonetheless, its rich palette and emotive force incited critics who saw it as a challenge to the classical tradition represented by David's and Delacroix's arch rival, Ingres. During his late twenties and thirties, Delacroix painted the defining pictures of his career and enjoyed many lucrative commissions. His monumental allegory, *Liberty Leading the People*, inspired by street fighting during the 1830 July Revolution, earned him the Legion of Honor. In 1832, Delacroix traveled to Morocco, Spain, and Algeria, whose blazing light and colors provided him with material for the rest of his life. His sketchbooks and paintings from this time would later inspire Matisse and Renoir. By the 1840s, Delacroix had become a sought-after guest at Paris's fashionable salons, where he mingled with friends such as Baudelaire, George Sand, and Frédéric Chopin. In 1857, he moved to his final studio on the Left Bank, just steps away from the murals he was completing at Saint-Sulpice church, where he worked diligently until his death in 1863.

Eugène Delacroix: *Self-portrait*, Musée du Louvre, Paris; Réunion des Musées Nationaux.

Delacroix in Paris
1857–1863
Storm in the Heart

"My new home is really charming. I felt rather depressed, after dinner, at finding myself transplanted, but I gradually became reconciled and went to bed quite happy," Eugène Delacroix confided in his journal. "I awoke next morning to find the sun shining in the most welcoming way on the houses opposite my window. The view on to the little garden, and the cheerful look of the studio continue to give me great pleasure."

In December of 1857, the great Romantic painter moved from his studio on rue Notre Dame de Lorette, on Paris's Right Bank, into what would become his last apartment and studio on the Left Bank, where he had spent much of his youth. Seriously ill from chronic laryngitis and persistent coughs and colds, the aging artist wanted to be closer to the church of Saint-Sulpice, where he was decorating the Chapel of the Holy Angels. This exhausting project required all his diminishing strength.

A friend had found these accommodations tucked away behind a stately red-brick façade in a courtyard off the tranquil Place de Furstenberg, one of the loveliest squares in Paris. A studio was promptly constructed in the small garden adjacent to the apartment. Once settled, Delacroix informed a relative that his garden was "reasonably well kept up and induces me to breathe fresh air in between sessions of work."

To his cousin and sometime mistress, Josephine de Forget, he announced: "I think I shall be very happy here. The rooms are much bigger than in my former apartment and this pleases me greatly. I hear no noise, which is another major point for a man who stays at home so much."

For years, Delacroix had been vilified as a savage and madman, who "hurled buckets of color against the canvas" and "painted with a drunken broom," according to some

Delacroix's last apartment and studio were on the charming Place de Furstenberg (opposite) on the Left Bank of Paris. Here, near the École des Beaux-Arts, where he had studied four decades earlier, the aging artist came to live and work. Today, the building houses the Musée Eugène Delacroix.

Personal mementos in the studio include leather drums and boots, colorful ceramics, swords, and a carved and painted Moroccan chest, all of which Delacroix acquired during his journey in North Africa, as well as letters to friends such as George Sand.

critics. "Thus it is that geniuses are greeted at their dawn," the critic Théophile Gautier wrote in the painter's defense. But now the revolutionary colorist was recognized as one of France's foremost painters.

The same year he moved to this studio he was elected at last to the Académie des Beaux-Arts after seven unsuccessful tries. A satisfied but exhausted Delacroix retreated from the hectic social life of salons, dinner parties, visits to relatives, concerts, and operas, and settled into a solitary existence, determined to conserve his energies and devote himself exclusively to his work. When he was not at Saint-Sulpice, he divided his time between his new studio and his modest country house, where he took long walks and sketched.

It was this image of the lone, work-driven genius who was at the same time a man of elaborate social grace and courtesy that awed the young Symbolist painter Odilon Redon, who followed Delacroix home from a ball given by Emperor Napoleon III at the Hotel de Ville in 1859. "He was as beautiful as a tiger, the same pride, the same finesse, the same strength," Redon enthused. "When he left the ball . . .

Delacroix's palette and paint table are on display in his studio.

I still wanted to see more of him, so we walked behind him through the streets . . . But when he reached the house on the Right Bank where he had lived for so many years, he seemed to realize that he had taken his way toward it out of habit, and he turned back and walked, still slowly and pensively, through the city and across the river, to the rue de Furstenberg."

Noted for his brilliant wit and elegant appearance, Delacroix had fierce eyes, thick, dark hair, and a feline expression, according to Gautier, who likened him to an educated Indian maharajah. Baudelaire observed that Delacroix "was like the crater of a volcano artistically hidden

by bouquets of flowers." He had "easily twenty different ways of uttering 'mon cher monsieur,' which to the trained ear denoted an intriguing range of feelings."

Delacroix's apartment and studio now house the Musée Eugène Delacroix. At the top of the grand staircase, a plaster bust of the master greets the visitor with his characteristic aristocratic reserve. This bust also served as a model for the bronze monument now in the nearby Luxembourg Gardens, one of the painter's favorite haunts. The entrance hall, which in Delacroix's day was outfitted with a green velvet-uphol-stered oak bench, a rounded glass lantern, and copper coat hooks, opens into an intimate living room adorned with the artist's watercolors and drawings of the Normandy coast, Paris scenes, and horses and Arabs inspired by his journey to North Africa in 1832.

Heavy olive drapes and fabric-covered walls lend a hushed solemnity to the room, once hung with garnet velvet curtains that protected the frail artist from the cold. Other furnishings included a mahogany armchair upholstered in flowered damask, a suite of rosewood furniture, an Indian-style writing desk, and four Louis XV-style gilded bronze

Delacroix's studio overlooks a courtyard garden. Inside (opposite), artworks from the collection of the Musée Eugène Delacroix are displayed in rotation.

candelabras, among other pieces, according to an inventory of possessions taken after his death.

In the bedroom to the left, where Delacroix died in 1863, the crimson fabric-covered walls are hung with portraits of the painter's family and Jenny Le Guillou, his faithful Breton housekeeper who nursed him through his final days. Although Delacroix's friends often complained of her fierce protectiveness, "She is blind devotion in person, she watches over my life and my time like a soldier on guard," said Delacroix, who never married.

Also displayed here are watercolors of oriental scenes and drawings illustrating works by Byron and the French Romantic writer Chateaubriand. Delacroix's painting of the mahogany bed in which he died occupies a corner niche near the marble fireplace, along with bronze medallions of his parents. An intricately carved pedestal table and a small chair with orange velvet cushions are among the few furnishings in the apartment that actually belonged to Delacroix, whose personal belongings were auctioned immediately after his death.

A mahogany bureau and green velvet récamier contribute to the atmosphere of neoclassical elegance in which he lived. In Delacroix's time the decor included an English rosewood dresser, an Empire-style armchair, a mahogany settee upholstered in velvet, a mirrored cupboard, and more than one hundred leather- and paper-bound books. Twill window curtains and door curtains made of Algerian rep kept out the drafts.

The library to the right of the living room was used as a waiting room for visitors as well as a passageway to the adjoining garden studio. Works by Delacroix displayed here include a drawing of a scene from a Sir Walter Scott novel and a vigorous pen-and-ink study of a lion, which recalls his love for the exotic. There is also a photograph of a pensive and dignified Delacroix. A large oak desk that once belonged to Baudelaire has replaced Delacroix's, which was surrounded by four hundred books that served as raw material for his art. The works of Racine, Voltaire, and Stendhal were among his favorites.

Delacroix's dining room, just off the apartment's entrance, has been transformed into a research center that can be visited by appointment. His housekeeper lived in an adjacent room, now used to store art works.

An iron staircase extends from the library through the garden to the cavernous, light-infused studio, built according to Delacroix's specifications with an austere beige stucco façade and southern exposed windows. Here he worked incessantly until his final days, often without stopping to eat or shave, interrupted only by his recurrent throat illness, fevers, and migraines.

In his later paintings, an increasingly introspective Delacroix returned to the subject matter of his early works— landscapes, the hunt, wild animals in combat, and scenes from literature, mythology, and religion.

The grand murals at Saint-Sulpice, completed in 1861, occupied most of his time and became the crowning achievement of his career. "I have been working all day long. What a good life! . . . Painting, it's true, like the most exacting of mistresses, harasses and torments me in a hundred ways. For the last four months I have been getting up at dawn and hurrying off to this enchanting work as though I were rushing to throw myself at the feet of a beloved mistress," Delacroix marveled about his work on the murals. His now-famous journal was one of Monet's favorite books.

He decorated the Chapel of the Holy Angels, on the right side of the church entrance, with biblical scenes that are recognized as the finest mural painting of his time. In *Jacob Wrestling with the Angel* and *Heliodorus Driven from the Temple* (on the walls) and *St. Michael Defeating the Devil* (on the ceiling), Delacroix depicted the eternal struggle between good and evil through violent conflict, one of his favorite themes. These dramatic works are rooted in the lessons of the old masters, particularly Raphael, Titian, and Rubens, and Delacroix's lifelong study of nature.

In the studio, his easel stands mounted with an engraved self portrait. Nearby is a mahogany table that held his paints. His palette rests there as if he had just left it to step into the garden for some air.

"The sight of my palette freshly set out with colors all shining in their contrasts is enough to excite my enthusi-

asm," wrote Delacroix, who, according to a friend, worked in "an old jacket buttoned up to the chin, a large muffler round his neck, a cloth cap pulled over his ears, and a pair of thick felt slippers" because he was always shivering with cold.

Various drawings, lithographs, and small paintings by the artist from the museum's collection are displayed in rotation in the studio and throughout the apartment. Notable among those in the studio are various studies for his famous painting, *The Death of Sardanapalus*, which scandalized the Salon of 1827 with its turbulent eroticism and became a rallying cry for the Romantics.

"Delacroix was passionately in love with passion, but coldly determined to express passion as clearly as possible," wrote Baudelaire, who equated Romanticism with modern art in its "intimacy, spirituality, color, aspiration towards the infinite." Cézanne said that Delacroix had "the greatest palette of France, and no one beneath our skies possessed to a greater extent the vibration of color. We all paint through him."

By the summer of 1863, Delacroix had finally succumbed to his illness and spent his last hours in the care of his devoted Jenny, eating figs, cherries, and ice cream, and preparing his will. He died peacefully, according to one friend who was present at his bedside, "with that air of exotic aristocracy that brings to mind legendary Persian princes."

The art critic Théophile Silvestre offered his own moving testimony: "Delacroix died, almost smiling . . . a painter of great genius, who had the sun in his head and storms in his heart, who for forty years played the entire keyboard of human emotion, and whose grandiose, terrible, and delicate brushes passed from saints to warriors, from warriors to lovers, from lovers to tigers, and from tigers to flowers."

(Opposite) Eugène Delacroix: *Arabs Skirmishing in the Mountains* (1863), National Gallery of Art, Washington, Chester Dale Fund.

Gustave Moreau

Best known for mysterious paintings based on mythology, the Bible, and great works of literature, the iconoclastic Gustave Moreau was the last of the Romantic painters, a dreamer and visionary whose hallucinatory canvases evoke the furthest reaches of the imagination. Though he considered himself a history painter in the tradition of Ingres and Delacroix, he influenced Matisse and the Fauves, and has been hailed as a forefather to the Symbolists and such Surrealists as Max Ernst and Salvador Dali. His late works have been praised as precursors to Abstract Expressionism. Moreau was born in Paris in 1826 to an architect and a musician who lavished him with intellectual and financial support throughout his career. He studied at Paris's prestigious École des Beaux-Arts, where he concentrated on drawing and copied paintings in the Louvre, particularly those by Mantegna, Michelangelo, and Carpaccio. Admired during his lifetime, Moreau was disillusioned by his own era's emphasis on scientific and rational thought and its fascination with naturalism in art. Rather, he was inspired by ancient, medieval, and Renaissance art, and exotic cultures, and his work is noted for its exquisite craftsmanship, imaginative detail, and visual richness and complexity. Possessed of a keen intelligence and exuberant temperament, Moreau initially painted family portraits, landscapes, and Shakespearean subjects in the spirit of his admired older contemporaries, Delacroix and Chasseriau; Chasseriau became a good friend and lived near Moreau's studio on the place Pigalle. An elegantly-dressed dandy, Moreau attended the opera and theatre and sang in an accomplished tenor at Paris's fashionable salons. He exhibited at the Salon for the first time in 1852 with a *Pietà* that attracted considerable attention. That year, his parents bought him a house on the Right Bank, where he resided for forty-six years until his death in 1898 at age seventy-two, creating his epic, dreamlike masterpieces.

Gustave Moreau: *Self-portrait* (1872–1875), Musée Gustave Moreau, Paris.

(Opposite) Gustave Moreau: *Salomé Dancing* (c. 1876), Musée Gustave Moreau, Paris; Giraudon/Art Resource, New York.
This is a study for Moreau's celebrated painting *Salomé Dancing Before Herod*, now at the Los Angeles County Museum of Art. The tattoos on Salomé's body are designs for the jewels that cover her in the final version. Imbued with a mysterious eroticism, the painting entranced the writer Joris Karl Huysmans, who described it at length in his landmark novel, *Against Nature*.

Moreau in Paris
1852–1898
Mystic Genius

"He is a mystic secluded in the center of Paris in a cell to which not even the noise of contemporary life can penetrate, and yet that noise is beating furiously at the gates of the cloister. Rapt in ecstasy, he sees entrancing visions glitter before his eyes . . . " the French writer Joris Karl Huysmans proclaimed of Gustave Moreau.

It was here in his townhouse on rue de La Rochefoucauld near the seedy Pigalle district that Moreau cultivated his image as the reclusive aesthete. "Moreau, the master sorcerer, . . . has smitten a whole generation of artists yearning today for other-worldliness and mysticism," wrote Jean Lorrain, one of the "decadent school" of French writers and Symbolist poets for whom Moreau had become a cult figure.

Intensely private, Moreau was as enigmatic as his lavishly decorative art, which he described as " . . . soaring off into sacred, unknown, mysterious lands." Free from financial pressures thanks to his parents' support and the patronage of loyal dealers and collectors, Moreau, who never married, long planned to create a museum in his name to secure his posthumous reputation.

As early as age thirty-six, Moreau reflected: "I think of my death and of the fate of all these works and compositions I have taken such trouble to collect. Separately they will perish, but taken as a whole they give an idea of what kind of an artist I was and in what kind of surroundings I chose to live my dreams."

It was not until shortly before his death, however, that Moreau actually set to work enlarging the Right Bank house where he had lived since 1852. He meticulously reorganized the first-floor apartment where his parents had lived, preserving its main rooms almost intact. He also transformed the second and third floors into two large exhibition galleries for his art.

A dramatic focal point of the Musée Gustave Moreau is the elegant spiral staircase (opposite), which leads visitors to the third-floor exhibition galleries.

Moreau lived for more than half his life in this townhouse on the Right Bank of Paris. It is now home to the Musée Gustave Moreau.

The artist himself lived and worked primarily in a small attic studio, no longer extant, where he stockpiled the canvases on which he worked intermittently as his moods dictated.

The museum, opened in 1903, houses an astonishing 14 thousand works that the artist bequeathed to the state. A perfectionist, he rarely was able to part with his paintings during his lifetime, and continually reworked them in a state of nervous excitement. Thousands of drawings, pastels, and watercolors displayed in wooden cabinets throughout the upstairs galleries and in the ground floor exhibition rooms offer a rare view of an artist in the act of creation. Most of the works on display, however, are either unfinished or are preparatory studies for the several hundred works

Moreau sold during his lifetime, and which now hang in other collections.

Over the years, the museum has captivated such illustrious visitors as the writer André Malraux and the Surrealists Salvador Dali and André Breton. "More than anything else, the museum for me was like a temple, as it ought to be, and a place of ill repute as . . . it could also be," Breton wrote in 1950. "I have always dreamed of breaking into it at night with a lantern to surprise the *Fairy with Griffins* in the shadow, and catch the signals flying from *The Suitors* to *The Apparition*, halfway between the exterior and inner eye brought to the point of incandescence."

"Gustave Moreau," wrote Salvador Dali, "is the most glorious and scatological of painters, pursuing a single aim fanatically: to see gold appear at the tip of his brush. . . . I recommend those I love to visit the museum, to go and sink into that penumbra where hover the constellations of

The paintings, drawings, pastels, and watercolors displayed on the third floor of the Musée Gustave Moreau are among the many thousands in the museum's collection.

The furnishings in Moreau's bedroom were meticulously arranged by the artist. Responding to criticism of the bourgeois character of the home, Moreau countered, "Do you think I don't know as well as you that the chandelier, the candlesticks, and most of the furniture here are valueless? But they suited my parents, and that's enough for me. When I want to see beautiful things, I go to the Louvre."

precious stones arising from the abyss of erotic . . . obsessions, like so many promises of an archangelic redemption." Because he arranged for many of his letters to be destroyed after his death, little is known about Moreau's personal life. Yet the museum provides a glimpse into his magical interior universe. An early photograph of the artist hangs in the pink wallpapered corridor beside works by other artists such as Poussin and Burne-Jones. Reproductions of works by Rembrandt, whom Moreau greatly admired, decorate the entrance to the family dining room, which displays engravings and photographs of paintings that Moreau sold during his lifetime.

A portrait of Moreau by Edgar Degas (center, above), who resided nearby, hangs above the desk in the bedroom, recalling the artists' friendship during Degas's formative years.

The close relationship between the artist and his mother, who managed her son's household, is glimpsed in his affecting watercolor portrait of her. Moreau wrote detailed explanations of his paintings for his mother after she lost her hearing and was devastated by her death in 1884. "I have been so stricken over the last eight months by sorrow and illness that I was obliged to stop working altogether," he lamented.

In the dining room, crimson embossed wallpaper and matching drapes provide a striking contrast to the pale-green wood paneling. Wicker dining chairs, a table covered with fringed embroidery, and a green velvet armchair are typical fin-de-siècle furnishings. Sixteenth- and 17th-century ceramics by Bernard Palissy, as well as Chinese and Turkish Iznik wares, sit atop a credenza. Although their colorful, intricate patterns echo the sumptuous detail of Moreau's paintings, some of which replicate these very motifs and colors, the bourgeois ambience of the room belies the painter's taste for the exotic.

In the adjacent bedroom, formerly the drawing room, are family portraits and the artist's early works, as well as photographs, engravings, drawings, and paintings by friends.

A portrait of Moreau by Degas, who resided nearby, hangs above his desk, recalling their friendship in Italy in 1857, when Moreau greatly influenced the younger painter. Their creative paths diverged, however, when Degas later allied himself with the Impressionists. Moreau made no secret of his dislike for this band of revolutionaries, whose celebration of the more mundane events of daily life contrasted to his view of art as a sacred ideal, heavily laden with symbolic meaning.

The poet Paul Valéry recounted a later meeting between the two formidable egos: "Moreau took him up one day by saying, 'Do you think you can revive art through dance?' 'And you, retorted Degas, do you think you can revive it through jewelry?'" Referring to the elaborate ornamentation of Moreau's paintings, Degas, on another occasion, sniped, "He wants to make us believe that the gods wore watch chains."

Furnished with a bronze floral chandelier, patterned blue wallpaper, gold drapes, tapestried chairs, and Sèvres porcelain, the room's centerpiece is the mahogany bed where Moreau's body was laid out after he died in 1898. This chamber, like the others, was meticulously arranged by Moreau himself in a delightful jumble that recalls the cluttered, eclectic quality of his paintings.

The formal black embroidered suit that the honored Moreau wore upon his election to the Académie des Beaux Arts now lies draped over a chair next to the bed. Another portrait of the artist hangs above one of a pair of bronze-mounted marquetry cabinets that flank the marble fireplace; a portrait of his mother adorns the wall to the left.

A glass showcase holds photographs, miniatures, and drawings of Moreau's family and close friends, including a portrait of his sister, Camille, that was drawn by Moreau as a child. Other items of sentimental significance include family jewelry and a tiny black velvet oriental slipper toy that had belonged to Camille, who died at age thirteen.

The last room, called the boudoir, is devoted to Moreau's "best and only friend," his cherished female companion, Alexandrine Dureux, whom he met in 1859 and installed in an apartment near here. Moreau was very secretive about their affair, which lasted until her death in 1890.

Photographs by Nadar of the stylish Dureux are displayed
here along with her furnishings and her collection of
Moreau's works, all of which returned to him after her death.
Luminous gilt-framed watercolors and paintings accompany
a decorative mantelpiece cover that he designed and she
embroidered. Other furnishings include Louis XVI-style
armchairs upholstered in yellow silk, ornate marquetry
furniture, a Swiss cuckoo clock, and a black handbag with
Dureux's initials.

The many medals awarded Moreau during his lifetime are
displayed on the landing leading up to the second and third
floor galleries. Here, his massive canvases gleam in the natural
light flooding upon them. Apollo, the Muses, Hercules,
Prometheus, Moses, Salomé, and a host of other mythological
and biblical figures are rendered in elaborate detail.

As one climbs the elegant spiral staircase, the dazzling
Jupiter and Semelé is the first painting to meet the eye. One
of Moreau's last and best pictures, which he described as a
"hymn to divinity," it later inspired the Surrealists. Nearby
are *The Life of Humanity*, whose nine panels of mythological
and biblical figures reenact history, and *Orpheus on the Tomb
of Eurydice*, an expressionist masterpiece that the despairing
Moreau, identifying himself with the mythological poet who
suffered a similar fate, painted after the death of his mistress.

An eclectic and scholarly artist, Moreau loved lavish
effects. He accessorized his paintings with jewelry, lush
vegetation, architectural remnants, and chimerical figures,
and borrowed ideas from such diverse sources as Ovid, La
Fontaine, illustrated periodicals, illuminated manuscripts,
Renaissance paintings, and Persian prints. He made frequent
visits to Paris's art and natural history museums to research
his imagery.

Moreau wrote that his aim as an artist was to "render
visible . . . the inner flashes of insight which . . . have something divine in their apparent meaninglessness and which,
as conveyed by . . . pure painting, open up really magical,
I may say even sublime, horizons."

Esteemed during his lifetime by an elite group of collectors and admirers, among them Proust and Flaubert, and the

young Symbolist painter Odilon Redon, the highly sensitive Moreau nevertheless suffered the wrath of critics who denounced his paintings as overly literary, excessively decorated "theatre sets." Others discredited him as an "admirable lunatic" and "smoker of opium."

In Moreau's defense, the critic Théophile Gautier retorted: "The qualities are so great! It needs so much talent, learning, intelligence, and exquisiteness to delude ourselves and achieve success like this!"

As the years passed, Moreau became ever more reclusive, refusing to exhibit his work, though he continued to receive official recognition as well as commissions. In the early 1880s, he compulsively began to revise many of the paintings in his studio, some of which were started three decades earlier. He enlarged them, added details, and stenciled over his figures with tattoo-like patterns. He came to view few works as completed.

He worked steadfastly through his final days, seldom leaving his studio. Even when confined to bed, he continued to fill his sketchbooks with drawings and commentaries on his work.

Moreau died of stomach cancer in 1898 at age seventy-two, secure in the knowledge that he had become the visual poet of his time. "I have found an inexpressible joy in a passionate attachment to my art and in ceaseless work. I have had my reward and I ask for no more," he declared a few hours before his death.

Paris

❧ Apartment and Studio of Eugène Delacroix

Musée National Eugène Delacroix
6, rue de Furstenberg
75006 Paris
Tel: (33) 01 44 41 86 50
Fax: (33) 01 43 54 36 70
Guided tours: (33) 01 40 13 46 46
Métro: St-Germain-des-Près
Delacroix's last apartment and studio, where he lived from 1857 to his death in 1863, now houses a museum dedicated to his life and work.
HOURS: Open every day but Tuesday, January 1, May 1, and December 25 from 9:30 a.m. to 5 p.m. (Ticket counter closes at 4:30 p.m.). A reservation is required for group visits. There is a small gift shop and bookstore. A free brochure with a map lists Delacroix's former residences and studios in Paris.
ENTRY FEE: 30 francs; 23 francs for those under age 26; free under 18.

❧ Left Bank Sites

Saint-Sulpice
Place Saint-Sulpice
75006 Paris
Métro: St-Sulpice
The Left Bank's largest church, where Hemingway and Faulkner attended mass in the 1920s, this classical structure is distinguished by two square towers and is most notable for Delacroix's exquisite murals in the Chapel of the Holy Angels, just inside the entrance to the right. Delacroix's last major work, undertaken from 1849 to 1863, these three paintings have been hailed by critics as the pinnacle of his art. The left wall depicts *Jacob Wrestling with the Angel*; the right shows *Heliodorus Driven from the Temple*. The ceiling is decorated with *St. Michael Vanquishing*

Lucifer. Based on biblical stories about the conflict between good and evil, these murals combine Delacroix's careful nature studies with the lessons of the old masters (particularly Raphael, Rubens, and Titian), whom he strove to emulate. They shine with the dynamic movement and expressive color that are his hallmarks. Delacroix worked with assistants on all of his great mural projects. He trained them to paint the backgrounds while he designed the composition, worked out the colors, and retouched the nearly completed painting in the traditon of the old masters. "Some days the master would be absolutely silent as a carp, at other times he would seize a prepared palette and would work as one possessed," according to one assistant, Pierre Andrieu, who noted that Delacroix painted the hat and cloak in front of *Jacob and the Angel* in twenty-two minutes; left it to dry for sixteen days, and repainted it in sixteen minutes.

Église Saint-Denis-du-Saint-Sacrèment
68, rue de Turenne
75003 Paris
Métro: St-Sebastien OR Froissart
This church in the Marais houses one of Delacroix's least known works—an 1844 mural of a *Pietà*, in which the Virgin Mary bears her Son's crucified body. Situated in a high, dark corner, its rich coloring and symmetrical composition reveal a debt to Renaissance art. "This masterpiece digs a deep furrow of human melancholy," Baudelaire proclaimed.

Église Saint-Paul-Saint-Louis
99, rue Saint-Antoine
75004 Paris
Métro: St-Paul
One of Delacroix's earliest paintings, *The Agony in the Garden*, shown at the Salon of 1827–1828, can be found high up on a wall in

this Baroque church in the Marais, not far from Église Saint-Denis.

Palais du Luxembourg Senate
15, rue de Vaugirard
75006 Paris
Tel: (33) 01 42 34 20 60
     (33) 01 44 61 20 89
Métro: Luxembourg
In 1840 Delacroix decorated the half-dome and cupola in the library of the Senate in the Italianate Luxembourg Palace, which was commissioned by Maria de'Medici in 1615 to remind her of her native Tuscany. Based on Canto IV of Dante's *Inferno*, the cupola decoration depicts great figures from antiquity like Dante, Virgil, Socrates, Aristotle, and Caesar, who symbolize the achievements of the human spirit.
HOURS: Visits are generally permitted the first Sunday of each month.

Musée du Louvre Galerie d'Apollon
75001 Paris
Tel: (33) 01 40 20 51 51
Métro: Palais-Royal OR Musée du Louvre
Delacroix decorated the ceiling of the Galerie d'Apollon in the Louvre in 1850 with a scene portraying Apollo slaying the serpent Python, symbolic of the triumph of light over darkness. The long hours spent on scaffoldings to complete his public commissions took a considerable toll on Delacroix's delicate health.

Assemblée Nationale
Salon du Roi (also called Salon Delacroix) and Bibliothèque
33, bis quai d'Orsay
75007 Paris
Tel: (33) 01 40 63 99 99
(Call for an appointment)
Métro: Assemblée Nationale
In 1833, at the age of 35, Delacroix received a commission to decorate the Salon du Roi (King's throne room) in the Palais-Bourbon (now the National Assembly) which func-

Eugène Delacroix: *Jacob Wrestling with the Angel* (1853–1863), Saint-Sulpice, Paris; Giraudon/Art Resource, New York.

Italy and the Arts, which illustrate the delicate balance between civilization and barbarism, one of the great painter's favorite themes. For his public commissions, Delacroix aimed to integrate his work with the existing architecture, with particular emphasis on a unified color scheme that expressed the vitality of his vision.

Père Lachaise Cemetery

10, avenue du Père Lachaise
75020 Paris
Tel: (33) 01 46 36 37 52
Métro: Père Lachaise OR Gambetta
Delacroix is buried here in Paris's largest and most famous cemetery. His grave is marked by a black stone, monumental and classical in proportion. Also laid to rest along the rambling walkways and rolling hills of this beautifully landscaped urban oasis are many illustrious artists and writers, including Proust, Molière, Balzac, Colette, Oscar Wilde, Ingres, Corot, Seurat, and Ernst, as well as Rosa Bonheur and Charles-François Daubigny. An illustrated map can be purchased on site for 10 francs.

✤ Left Bank Dining

There are many excellent, historic restaurants and cafes in the vicinity of the Delacroix Museum. A few personal favorites are:

Cafe les Deux Magots

6, place Saint-Germain-des-Près
75006 Paris
Tel: (33) 01 45 48 55 25
Fax: (33) 01 45 49 31 29
Métro: St-Germain-des-Près
Since 1885, this elegant cafe has played an important role in the cultural life of Paris. Over the years, it has been frequented by numerous artists and writers including Rimbaud, Mallarmé, Picasso, Léger, Hemingway, Sartre, and de Beauvoir. Picasso met his muse and model

tions as a writing and reception area for members of the legislature. On the four friezes above the doorways in the Salon du Roi are allegories of the components of government—justice, agriculture, industry, and war. Allegories of the rivers of France adorn the piers dividing the room. From 1838 to 1847, Delacroix and his assistants painted the library of the Chamber of Deputies. The five small cupolas portray allegories of five areas of human achievement—poetry, theology, literature, philosophy, and natural history. In the half-domes Delacroix depicted the dawn of civilization and its collapse with *Orpheus Bringing the Art of Peace to Primitive Greece*, and *Attila and his Hordes Overrunning*

Dora Maar here. Simone de Beauvoir read and worked on a novel here. A magnet for the Surrealists and Existentialists during the early 20th century, it still attracts luminaries from the art and literary worlds. The mahogany, mirrored interior offers a cozy ambience in which to socialize, people watch, or simply read a book. Crowds are the only deterrent, particularly during warmer months, when the outdoor terrace buzzes with activity. Typical cafe fare includes salads, sandwiches, cheeses, omelets, quiche, and pastries. Expect to pay extra for the cultural cachet and atmosphere—well worth it.

Cafe de Flore

172, boulevard Saint-Germain
75006 Paris
Tel. (33) 01 45 48 55 26
Fax: (33) 01 45 44 33 39
Métro: St-Germain-des-Prés
Like its neighbor, Les Deux Magots, Cafe de Flore is a Left Bank cultural icon. This welcoming cafe, with its faded Art Deco interior of red banquettes, mirrors, and mahogany, was a gathering place for André Breton and the Surrealists, Picasso, Chagall, and Sartre and de Beauvoir, who used it as a study, writing from morning to night. It is now a bastion for poets, journalists, and filmmakers. Typical cafe fare. The hot chocolate is excellent.

Brasserie Lipp

151, boulevard Saint-Germain
75006 Paris
Tel: (33) 01 45 48 53 91
Métro: St-Germain-des-Prés
Located across the street from Cafe de Flore and Les Deux Magots, Brasserie Lipp has retained its authentic Belle Époque interior, with dark wood furniture, mirrors, leather banquettes, high painted ceilings, and ceramic tile walls. Its illustrious visitors have included Thornton Wilder, Hemingway, who wrote about it in *A Moveable Feast*,

and former French president François Mitterand. It has always been a favorite with writers, actors, politicians, and businessmen. Dishes include roast chicken, grilled lamb chop, smoked salmon, grilled beef, and Alsatian sausage and sauerkraut. Prices range from 44 francs for cream-of-vegetable soup to 270 francs for caviar.

Cafe de la Mairie

8, place Saint-Sulpice
75006 Paris
Tel: (33) 01 43 26 67 82
Métro: St-Sulpice
This quiet little cafe on the leafy square near Saint-Sulpice church is less expensive than its Saint-Germain neighbors, but just as steeped in literary history. From the mid-1920s onward, it was a favorite haunt of Henry Miller, Camus, Sartre, de Beauvoir, Beckett, and Djuna Barnes, who set part of her novel, *Nightwood*, here. Hemingway, Faulkner, and Fitzgerald were among the many writers who lived in the neighborhood. Typical cafe fare. Terrace dining when weather permits.

La Palette

43, rue de Seine
75006 Paris
Tel: (33) 01 43 26 68 15
Métro: Odéon OR Mabillon
There is no better place on the Left Bank to while away an afternoon than this cozy, rustic cafe that has attracted thousands of artists and writers since the turn of the century. Among its notable habitués were Henry Miller, Sartre, and de Beauvoir (all of whom lived up the street at Hôtel La Louisiane). Situated on a tree-lined square just north of Saint-Germain-des-Prés near the famed École des Beaux-Arts, and surrounded by galleries and artist's studios, La Palette has one of the loveliest sidewalk locations in Paris. Outdoor dining is de rigueur in warm weather. Among

the writers and artists who settled in the neighborhood were Gertrude Stein and Alice B. Toklas, who lived at 5, rue Christine. Picasso painted Guernica at 7, rue des Grands-Augustins. Balzac lived at 17, rue Visconti, while Natalie Barney held her famous salons in the 1920s at 20, rue Jacob. La Palette serves typical cafe fare at lower prices than its Saint-Germain counterparts.

Le Procope

13, rue de l'Ancienne Comédie
75006 Paris
Tel: (33) 01 40 46 79 00
Fax: (33) 01 40 46 79 09
Métro: Odéon
Founded in 1686, the oldest cafe in Paris (formerly Cafe Procope) was long a gathering place for artists, writers, and politicians. Closely linked with 18th-century revolutionary ideas, it was frequented by Robespierre, Marat, and Danton, as well as Benjamin Franklin and Thomas Jefferson. The philosphers Voltaire and Rousseau also met here; Voltaire's table has been preserved upstairs. In the nineteenth century its customers included Hugo, Balzac, Cézanne, and George Sand. Le Procope is now a restaurant serving dishes such as grilled lobster, veal, lamb, filet of beef, fresh salmon, shrimp, and oysters, which range in price from 60 francs to 198 francs.
HOURS: Open every day from 11 a.m. to 1 a.m.

Restaurant Polidor

41, rue Monsieur-le-Prince
75006 Paris
Tel: (33) 01 43 26 95 34
Métro: Odéon
Opened in 1845, this charming restaurant near the Sorbonne in the Latin Quarter serves simple, inexpensive bistro food in an old-world interior outfitted with wood paneling and cabinets, antique mirrors, and long tables. Rimbaud and Verlaine were among its notable 19th-century patrons, while the

young James Joyce, who lived around the corner on rue Corneille, dined here in the early 1900s. Menus ranging from 55 francs to 100 francs offer roast chicken, pork curry, salmon, hen in white sauce, blood sausage, and spinach salad, among other items.
HOURS: Open for lunch from 12 p.m to 2:30 p.m.; dinner from 7 p.m. to 12:30 a.m. (Sundays until 11 p.m.)

❧ Left Bank Accommodations

Hôtel d'Angleterre
44, rue Jacob
75006 Paris
Tel: (33) 01 42 60 34 72
Fax: (33) 01 42 60 16 93
Métro: St-Germain-des-Près
In the heart of Saint-Germain-des-Près, this charming small hotel, formerly known as Hôtel Jacob et d'Angleterre, housed the British Embassy in the 18th century. Benjamin Franklin, John Adams, and John Jay negotiated the treaty for American independence with the British here. During the 1920s numerous American expatriates, including Djuna Barnes and Ernest and Hadley Hemingway, rented rooms here. A quiet indoor garden, 19th-century staircase, and spacious rooms decorated with period furniture make this three-star hotel an excellent choice. It is just steps away from the Delacroix Museum. Room rates range from 650 francs for a double room to 1150 francs for a deluxe room. Breakfast is 55 francs extra.

Relais Christine
3, rue Christine
75006 Paris
Tel: (33) 01 40 51 60 80
Fax: (33) 01 40 51 60 81
Métro: Odéon
Located just a few blocks away from Hôtel d'Angleterre, the beautiful Relais Christine is housed in a mansion whose history dates back to the early 17th century. There is a central courtyard, rear garden, a wood-paneled lobby decorated with antiques, and fifty-one elegantly appointed rooms and suites. The dining room is situated in a vaulted basement (with a great fireplace) that bears traces of its medieval heritage as a monastery. Couched at the end of a narrow street, this four-star hotel has preserved the intimacy of the private residence it once was. It is a haven of tranquility in the bustling Saint-Germain-des-Près district. Room rates are 1650 francs to 1800 francs for a single room; 1850 francs to 2100 francs for a double; 2400 francs to 4000 francs for suites. Buffet breakfast is 135 francs extra; continental breakfast is 110 francs.

L'Hôtel
13, rue des Beaux-Arts
75006 Paris
Tel: (33) 01 44 41 99 00
Fax: (33) 01 43 25 64 81
Métro: St-Germain-des-Près
Located on an historic, gallery-lined street across from the famed École des Beaux-Arts, the invitingly eccentric L'Hôtel is perhaps best known as the last abode of Oscar Wilde, who died here on November 30, 1900 at age forty-six, exiled from England after his imprisonment. The plaque on the door to his room (reconstituted with Wilde's furniture) reads that "he died here beyond his means." "I can't bear this wallpaper," Wilde supposedly remarked before his death. "One of us will have to go." The former Hôtel d'Alsace, as it was called then, was much less luxurious than its present incarnation. Now one of the most upscale establishments on the Left Bank, this hotel has hosted the likes of Robert De Niro, Elizabeth Taylor, Richard Burton, and other celebrities. A dizzying spiral staircase dominates the lobby, while the winter garden serves as a piano bar adorned with a fountain, oriental rugs, modern paintings and sculpture, and the pièce de résistance—a live tree growing through the roof. Twenty-seven rooms are sumptuously decorated with Venetian marble bathrooms and antiques in various styles ranging from Art Deco to Empire. Room rates range from 600 francs to 2500 francs for doubles; 1700 francs to 3600 francs for suites. Breakfast is 100 francs extra.

Relais Saint-Germain
9, carrefour de l'Odéon
75006 Paris
Tel: (33) 01 44 27 07 97
Fax: (33) 01 46 33 45 30
Métro: Odéon
One of the loveliest hotels on the Left Bank, the four-star Relais Saint-Germain occupies a 17th-century house in the heart of Saint-Germain-des-Près. Twenty-two spacious rooms, several with original wood-beamed ceilings and walls, are beautifully decorated with antiques and luxurious fabrics. Opened in 1986, this hotel is owned by interior designers Christiane and Gilbert Laipsker. Old-world charm blends with modern conveniences such as large marble bathrooms. The hotel's wine bar once catered to Man Ray, Picasso, and Joyce. Room rates are 1,290 francs for singles; 1560 francs for doubles; deluxe rooms with a sitting room and large foyer are 1800 francs; terrace suites are 2050 francs. Breakfast included.

Hôtel Récamier
3, bis place Saint-Sulpice
75006 Paris
Tel: (33) 01 43 26 04 89
Fax: (33) 01 46 33 27 73
Métro: St-Sulpice OR Mabillon
For those on a tighter budget, the two-star Hôtel Récamier offers simple, clean rooms ranging from 620 francs (with shower) to 650 and 700 francs (with bath). It occupies a quiet corner of the lovely Saint-Sulpice square near the church. Gertrude Stein and Alice B. Toklas

lived here briefly, and Djuna Barnes also wrote about the hotel in her novel, *Nightwood*.

♫ House and Studio of Gustave Moreau

Musée Gustave Moreau
14, rue de la Rochefoucauld
75009 Paris
Tel: (33) 01 48 74 38 50
Fax: (33) 01 48 74 18 71
Métro: Trinité
The Moreau Museum is located in Paris's 9th arrondissement, near the Pigalle red-light district. It incorporates the family's first-floor apartment and spacious galleries filled with thousands of his paintings, watercolors, and drawings, as well as an extensive archive, including notebooks, letters, a library, and studio props, which can be visited by appointment.
HOURS: Open on Mondays and Wednesdays from 11 a.m. to 5:15 p.m.; other days from 10 a.m. to 12:45 p.m. and 2 p.m. to 5:15 p.m. Closed Tuesdays.
ENTRY FEE: 22 francs; 15 francs for students, youths under age 25, and groups of ten or more; free for those under age 18.

♫ Right Bank Sites

Sand, Chopin, Delacroix, and Géricault all resided at various times in this artistic and literary district, known as Nouvelle Athènes (New Athens) during the Romantic era. Nouvelle Athènes spans the rues de la Rochefoucauld (where the Moreau Museum is located) and Tour-des-Dames, and the rues Blanche and Saint-Lazare. The apartments of Sand and Chopin are marked by plaques and located off rue Taitbout (one block from rue de la Rochefoucauld) in the lovely square d'Orléans, dominated by a fountain and a grand white and yellow neoclassical building.

Chopin lived at #9 from 1842 to 1849, while Sand lived across the courtyard at #5 from 1842 to 1847. The novelist recalls her apartment in *The Story of My Life*: "We only needed to cross one large courtyard, a green and sandy area which was always kept clean, to join the gatherings held in her home (that of Madame Marliani, the wife of the Spanish Consul) or in mine, or in Chopin's when he felt inclined to play for us."

Spread out on a small marble-topped table in the boudoir of Gustave Moreau's living quarters are yellowed newspaper reviews of his work, which his mistress, Alexandrine Dureux, lovingly saved.

In 1844, Delacroix lived at #54 on the nearby rue Notre-Dame de Lorette. The streets around here were renowned as the haunts of Paris's seamy underworld, which Émile Zola recounted in his novel, *Nana* (1880). In it, the courtesan Nana's friend, Satin, lives in a little room on the rue de la Rochefoucauld. Writers such as Zola, Maupassant, and Hugo all lived in this area during the last half of the nineteenth century.

The 9th arrondisement was also noted for its literary cafes, including La Taverne Anglaise at 24, rue d'Amsterdam (not far from the poet Mallarmé's home on rue de Rome, where he held his famous Tuesday salons); Restaurant Trapp at 109, rue Saint-Lazare, where writers including Zola, Flaubert, and Maupassant founded the Naturalist movement in literature; and the Brasserie des Martyrs at 9, rue des Martyrs (near the church of Notre-Dame de Lorette), one of the intellectual havens of mid-nineteenth century Paris, whose illustrious clientele included Courbet and Baudelaire.

Musée de la Vie Romantique

16, rue Chaptal
75009 Paris
Métro: St-Georges OR Place Blanche OR Place Pigalle
Tel: (33) 01 48 74 95 38
Fax: (33) 01 48 74 28 42
Housed in the former residence of painter Ary Scheffer (1795–1858), a close friend of writer George Sand (1804–76), this charming little museum evokes the famous art and literary salons Scheffer held here in the 1830s. His illustrious guests included Sand, Liszt, Chopin, Géricault, Delacroix, Dickens, and Turgenev. The gold drawing room and the blue room, reconstituted from engravings of the period, recreate Sand's life at her country château at Nohant in the Indre, south of the Loire Valley, where she

lived with Chopin and entertained her friend, Delacroix. Her furniture, objets d'art, portraits, letters, paintings, and drawings by Sand herself, as well as her jewelry and other personal belongings, comprise the largest Sand collection (more than 170 items), bequeathed to the city of Paris by her granddaughter. Best known for her depictions of peasants and provincial life in works such as *The Pool of Evil* (1846) and *The Foundling* (1847–48), Sand launched the beginning of the regional novel in France. Also on display are drawings and pastels by Delacroix and two portraits and paintings of literary subjects by Scheffer. In the two light-flooded studios, Scheffer received and made portraits of the important figures of his time. Temporary exhibitions are devoted to the great Romantics like Liszt, Byron, and Delacroix, as well as lesser-known artists. A tree-lined lane leads to this yellow Italian-style house typical of the French Restoration period. Nestled in a secluded courtyard with a lovely garden, the museum is rarely crowded. It is just steps away from the Moreau Museum.
HOURS: Open Tuesdays through Sundays from 10 a.m. to 5:40 p.m. Closed Mondays and holidays.
ENTRY FEE: 17.50 francs

Montmartre Cemetery

Métro: Blanche
Moreau is buried here in the family vault near his mistress, Alexandrine Dureux. His grave is marked by a white cement column topped with a bronze urn, which could easily double as an architectural motif in one of his paintings. Degas, Stendhal, and Gautier, among other artists and writers, are also laid to rest here. To reach the cemetery, take boulevard de Clichy to rue Caulaincourt. Turn right, and walk toward the cemetery and down a flight of stairs to the entrance. Maps are posted throughout the cemetery.

Drouot

9, rue Drouot
75009 Paris
Métro: Richelieu-Drouot
Tel: (33) 01 48 00 20 20
Fax: (33) 01 48 00 20 33
This large complex of salerooms is Paris's equivalent of an auction house, one of the oldest in the world. Located just off boulevard Montmartre, not far from the Moreau Museum, Drouot serves an organization of more than one hundred individual commissaires-priseurs. These auctioneers have enjoyed a comfortable monopoly on the French art market for hundreds of years, since foreign competition is prohibited by law. (That status may soon change as European trade barriers disappear.) More than 2,000 sales take place at Drouot each year, many of which are conducted simultaneously in any of its sixteen salerooms. Call for auction schedules and catalogues.

The streets around rue Drouot, including rue de la Grange Batelière and rue de Provence are crowded with art galleries and antiques shops specializing in everything from old master and 19th-century paintings to antiquities, rugs, jewelry, and French furniture.

Opera House

Place de l'Opéra
75009 Paris
Métro: Opéra
Tel: (33) 01 40 01 22 63 (information)
Tel: (33) 01 40 01 22 63 (guided tours)
One of the highlights of this famous attraction is the colorful auditorium ceiling painted by Marc Chagall in 1964, which depicts a whimsical view of Paris. The Palais Garnier was commissioned by Napoleon III as part of the great reconstruction project carried out by Baron Haussmann, the city planner who created the Paris we know

today. Designed by Moreau's contemporary, the architect Charles Garnier, and opened in 1875, the Paris Opera epitomizes the sumptuous decor and taste for excess that characterized Second Empire art. Moreau, whose paintings exhibit the same qualities, was very much a man of his time.

Gare Saint-Lazare
Located on rue Saint-Lazare, a few blocks from the Moreau Museum, this famous train station was immortalized in an 1877 series of paintings by Claude Monet. Trains depart here for his home in Giverny and van Gogh's last garret in Auvers-sur-Oise.

❧ Right Bank Dining

Au Petit Riche
25, rue Le Peletier
75009 Paris
Tel: (33) 01 47 70 68 68,
      (33) 01 47 70 86 50
Fax: (33) 01 48 24 10 79
Métro: Richelieu-Drouot
This elegant Belle Époque restaurant, a composite of wood paneling, mirrors, brass fixtures, and red banquettes, serves fine Loire Valley cuisine and wines. Lunch menus at 160 francs and dinner menus from 135 to 175 francs include smoked salmon, roast lamb, foie gras, terrine of duck, and roast veal, with a focus on hearty, earthy fare.
HOURS: Open for lunch from 12:15 p.m. to 2:30 p.m.; dinner from 7 p.m. to 12:15 a.m. Closed Sundays.

Restaurant American Chez Haynes
3, rue Clauzel
75009 Paris
Tel: (33) 01 48 78 40 63
Métro: St-Georges
Since 1949, the first African-American-owned restaurant in Paris has attracted such expatriates as Louis Armstrong, Richard Wright, and James Baldwin. Soul food includes barbecued spare ribs and chicken, cornbread, chitterlings, New Orleans red beans and sausage, and corn on the cob, priced at under 100 francs. Elizabeth Taylor, Richard Burton, and Marlon Brando have all made their way to this tiny restaurant on an obscure street a few blocks away from Pigalle's red-light district.
HOURS: Open Tuesday through Saturday from 7 p.m. to 12:30 a.m.

L'Auberge du Clou
30, avenue Trudaine
75009 Paris
Métro: Anvers
A rustic stucco and wood-beamed interior distinguishes this charming little restaurant situated a few blocks away from Chez Haynes. Reportedly a favorite haunt of the Impressionists, it offers traditional French dishes for under 100 francs.

Cafe de la Paix
12, boulevard des Capucines
75009 Paris
Tel: (33) 01 40 07 32 32
Métro: Opéra
This historic cafe, part of the luxurious Grand Hotel which opened in 1862, was one of the most popular, civilized gathering places in 19th-century Paris and a favorite destination for out-of-towners. It's Belle Époque character has attracted the likes of Flaubert, Balzac, Zola, Henry James, European royalty, President James Buchanan, and Charles De Gaulle. The cafe and Grand Hotel have appeared in many short stories and novels, including Hemingway's *The Sun Also Rises*, and Henry James's *The American*. Expect to pay higher prices here for typical cafe fare. The outdoor terrace is perfect for people watching.
HOURS: Open daily from 10 a.m to 1 a.m.

❧ Right Bank Accommodations

While there are many excellent hotels in the nearby Opéra area, the immediate vicinity of the Moreau Museum claims one hotel of special note.

Hôtel des Croisés
63, rue Saint Lazare
75009 Paris
Tel: (33) 01 48 74 78 24
Fax: (33) 01 49 95 04 43
Métro: St-Lazare
This two-star hotel is noteworthy for its combination of old-world ambience and modern convenience at reasonable prices. Twenty-seven spacious rooms and four suites (some with marble fireplaces) are furnished with Art Nouveau and Art Deco antiques. New bathrooms have been recently installed. An old iron elevator, marble columns, and decorative wood paneling distinguish the lobby and hallways. A rare find in a neighborhood that is not known for stellar accommodations, this gem rises above its two-star status. It is within walking distance to the Opéra and Gare Saint Lazare. Room rates range from 400 to 450 francs for singles; 450 to 480 francs for doubles; 550 francs for suites. Breakfast is 35 francs extra.

Museums in Paris with works by Moreau:
❧ **Musée du Louvre**
   (drawings department)
   The Apparition
❧ **Musée d'Orsay**
❧ **Musée du Petit Palais**

Museums in Paris with works by Delacroix:
❧ **Musée du Louvre**
   The Death of Sardanapalus,
   Liberty Leading the People
❧ **Musée d'Orsay**
❧ **Musée des Arts Décoratifs**
❧ **Musée Carnavalet**
❧ **Musée du Petit Palais**
❧ **Musée de la Vie Romantique**

Selected Bibliography

Claude Monet

Joyes, Claire: *Claude Monet: Life at Giverny*. New York: Vendôme Press, 1985.

Michels, Heide: *Monet's House: An Impressionist Interior*. New York: Clarkson Potter, 1997.

Monet's Years at Giverny: Beyond Impressionism. New York: The Metropolitan Museum of Art, 1978.

Patin, Sylvie: *Monet: The Ultimate Impressionist*. New York: Harry N. Abrams, Inc., 1993.

Tucker, Paul Hayes et al.: *Monet in the 20th Century*. Boston: Museum of Fine Arts and London: Royal Academy of Arts, 1998.

Van Der Kemp, Gerald: *Monet: A Visit to Giverny*. Versailles: Éditions Art Lys, 1998.

Charles-François Daubigny

Bouret, Jean: *The Barbizon School and 19th-Century French Landscape Painting*. Greenwich CT: The New York Graphic Society, 1973.

Fidell-Beaufort, Madeleine and Janine Bailly-Herzberg: *Daubigny*. Paris: Éditions Geoffroy-Dechaume, 1975.

Hoeber, Arthur: *The Barbizon Painters*. Freeport NY: Books For Libraries Press, 1969.

Lassalle, Christian: *Charles-François Daubigny*. Paris: Éditions du Valhermeil.

Vincent van Gogh

Bonafoux, Pascal: *Van Gogh: The Passionate Eye*. London: Thames and Hudson, 1992.

Hammacher, A.M.: *Vincent van Gogh: Genius and Disaster*. New York: Abradale Press/Harry N. Abrams, Inc., 1985.

McQuillan, Melissa: *Van Gogh*. London: Thames and Hudson, 1989.

Metzger, Rainer and Ingo F. Walther: *Van Gogh: The Complete Paintings, Volumes I and II*. Cologne: Taschen, 1993.

Pickvance, Ronald: *Van Gogh in Saint-Rémy and Auvers*. New York: The Metropolitan Museum of Art and Harry N. Abrams, Inc., 1986.

Schapiro, Meyer: *Vincent van Gogh*. New York: Abradale Press, 1994.

Jean-François Millet

Bouret, Jean: *The Barbizon School and 19th-Century French Landscape Painting*. Greenwich CT: New York Graphic Society, 1973.

Caille, Marie-Thérèse: *Ganne Inn: Municipal Museum of the Barbizon School*. Éditions Gaud, 1994.

Hoeber, Arthur: *The Barbizon Painters*. Freeport, NY: Books For Libraries Press, 1969.

Jean-François Millet. London: Arts Council of Great Britain, Hayward Gallery, 1976.

Pollock, Griselda: *Millet*. London: Oresko Books Ltd. and New York: The Two Continents Publishing Group, 1977.

Smith, Charles Sprague: *Barbizon Days*. Freeport, NY: Books For Libraries Press, 1969.

Rosa Bonheur

Ashton, Dore and Denise Hare Browne: *Rosa Bonheur: A Life and a Legend.* New York: The Viking Press, 1981.

Klumpke, Anna, translated by Gretchen van Slyke. *Rosa Bonheur: The Artist's (Auto) Biography.* Ann Arbor: The University of Michigan Press, 1997.

Rosa Bonheur: All Nature's Children. New York: Dahesh Museum, 1998.

Shriver, Rosalia: *Rosa Bonheur, With a Checklist of Works in American Collections.* Philadelphia: The Art Alliance Press, 1982.

Gustave Courbet

Clark, T.J.: *Image of the People: Gustave Courbet and the Second French Republic, 1848-1851.* Greenwich CT: New York Graphic Society, 1973.

Chu, Petra Ten-Doesschate: *Courbet in Perspective.* Englewood Cliffs, NJ: Prentice Hall, 1977.

Faunce, Sarah and Linda Nochlin: *Courbet Reconsidered.* New York: The Brooklyn Museum, 1988.

Fernier, Robert: *Gustave Courbet.* New York and Washington: Frederick A. Praeger Publishers, 1969.

Foucart, Bruno: *Courbet.* New York: Crown Publishers, Inc., 1977.

Rubin, James H.: *Courbet.* London: Phaidon Press Limited, 1997.

Eugène Delacroix

Delacroix: The Late Work. Paris: Réunion des Musées Nationaux and Philadelphia: Philadelphia Museum of Art, 1998.

Delacroix, Eugène: *The Journal of Eugène Delacroix.* London: Phaidon Press Limited, 1951, 1995.

Fitch, Noel Riley: *Walks in Hemingway's Paris.* New York: St. Martin's Press, 1992.

Fitch, Noel Riley: *Literary Cafés of Paris.* Starhill Press, 1989.

Johnson, Lee. *The Paintings of Eugène Delacroix: A Critical Catalogue, 1832 1863, Volume III.* Oxford: Clarendon Press, 1986.

Littlewood, Ian: *Paris: A Literary Companion.* London: John Murray Publishers Ltd., 1987.

Spector, Jack J.: *The Murals of Eugène Delacroix at Saint-Sulpice.* New York: Rutgers University and The College Art Association of America, 1967.

Trapp, Frank Anderson: *The Attainment of Delacroix.* Baltimore and London: The Johns Hopkins Press, 1970.

Wilson-Smith, Timothy: *Delacroix: A Life.* London: Constable and Company Limited, 1992.

The World of Delacroix. Amsterdam: Time-Life Books, 1966, 1984.

Gustave Moreau

Kaplan, Julius: *Gustave Moreau.* Los Angeles: Los Angeles County Museum of Art and Greenwich CT: New York Graphic Society, 1974.

Lacambre, Geneviève et al.: *Between Epic and Dream: Gustave Moreau.* Chicago: The Art Institute of Chicago and Princeton: Princeton University Press, 1999.

Mathieu, Pierre-Louis: *Gustave Moreau.* Boston: New York Graphic Society, 1976.

Mathieu, Pierre-Louis and Geneviève Lacambre: *The Gustave Moreau Museum.* Paris: Édition de la Réunion des Musées Nationaux, 1997.

Paladilhe, Jean and José Pierre: *Gustave Moreau.* New York and Washington: Praeger Publishers, 1972.

Travel books from The Little Bookroom

The Impressionists' Paris by Ellen Williams
Walking tours of the artists' studios, homes, and the sites they painted
This guidebook pairs some of the most beloved masterpieces
of Impressionism with the exact locations where they were
painted. Listings for restaurants, many dating from the
Impressionist era, round out the tours.
HARDCOVER $19.95 ISBN 0-9641262-2-2

Picasso's Paris by Ellen Williams
Walking tours of the artist's life in the city
A century after his arrival there as an unknown Spanish
teenager, Paris still bears the mark of Picasso's enduring presence. Four walking tours follow the painter from the gaslit
garrets of fin-de-siècle Paris to the Left Bank quarter where
he sat out the Nazi Occupation. Dining recommendations
include many of Picasso's favorite haunts.
HARDCOVER $19.95 ISBN 0-9641262-7-3

Here is New York by E. B. White
In the summer of 1949, E. B. White checked into The
Algonquin for the weekend and, sweltering in the summer
heat, wrote this remarkable essay. The New York Times has
chosen it as one of the ten best books ever written about
Manhattan. The New Yorker calls it "the wittiest essay, and
one of the most perceptive, ever done on the city."
With a new introduction by Roger Angell.
HARDCOVER $16.95 ISBN 0-9641262-7-3

Historic Restaurants of Paris by Ellen Williams
The vanished world of 19th-century Paris awaits behind
the doors of select restaurants and gourmet shops that have
delighted customers for more than a hundred years. From
tiny patisseries, cozy bistros, and rustic wine bars barely
known outside the quarter to bustling brasseries, elegant tea
salons, and world-famous cafés, this is an indispensible guide
to classic cuisine served in settings of startling beauty.
PAPERBACK $12.95 ISBN 1-892145-03-0

City Secrets Rome edited by Robert Kahn
Tour Rome in the company of its most passionate admirers
as the world's foremost artists, writers, architects, archaeologists,
and historians reveal their favorite discoveries in this ultimate
insider's guide. See the world's most magnificent art, architecture, and antiquities through the eyes of the people who
know and understand them best: a renowned painter shows
the way to a hidden garden, a poet laureate shares the address
of a little-known trattoria, a classicist suggests an ecclesiastical
shopping spree. Organized by area; with color maps,
vintage photos, and illustrations.
HARDCOVER $19.95 ISBN 0-9641262-04-9